STILLHOUSE
STORIES
TUNROOM TALES

STILLHOUSE STORIES TUNROOM TALES

GAVIN D. SMITH

ANGELS' SHARE

is an imprint of

Neil Wilson Publishing

www.nwp.co.uk

A catalogue record for this book is available from the British Library

The author has asserted his moral right under the Copyright,
Designs and Patents Act, 1988, as amended, to be identified as
the Author of this Work

Print edition ISBN: 978-1-906000-15-8
Ebook ISBN: 978-1-906000-16-5

Printed and bound in Poland

CONTENTS

ACKNOWLEDGEMENTS

MY THANKS GO TO THE SUBJECTS of this book, namely Norman Morrison, Boyo Norquoy, Jim Cryle, Gordon Dey, Rodney Burtt, Douglas Murray, John Peterson, Douglas Yeats, Ginger Willie, John Ramsay, John Grant and Stewart and Fred Laing. Furthermore quite a few pictures landed on my publisher's desk from a number of sources, some of which appear in the plate section herein.

For numerous images from the glory days of Glen Albyn and Glen Mhor, thanks to Rodney Burtt. I am also indebted to Gordon Bannerman, DK Cheung, Susie Davidson of The Edrington Group, Eddie McAffer of Morrison Bowmore Distillers Ltd, Christine McCafferty of The Diageo Archive, Dr Nicholas Morgan of Diageo, Robert Ransom of Glenfarclas Distillery, Pat Retson of The Edrington Group, Pat Roberts of Cognis PR, Jacqui Seargeant of John Dewar & Sons Ltd, Alan Sutton and Yvonne Thackeray of Chivas Brothers Ltd.

Finally, I want to thank anyone who has spent their working lives in the whisky industry as they have, knowingly or unknowingly, managed to help sustain one of Scotland's greatest products and are all part of Scotch whisky's remarkable history and heritage.

PREFACE

THESE DAYS THE WORLD OF Scotch whisky often seems to escape from its familiar confines within the 'Business' sections of newspapers and websites. Sometimes it makes mainstream headlines, usually as a result of yet another massive financial investment on behalf of one of the industry's major players, or a similarly positive statement from one of Scotland's smaller distillers.

Ongoing and hopefully long-term success across a diverse range of emerging markets, with Latin America as the crowning jewel, has given a rich impetus to all aspects of what is a source of national pride, status and employment.

However, the prosperous and optimistic Scotch whisky industry of today owes a huge debt to the skill, craftsmanship and enterprise of a great number of often unsung men and women. When we open a bottle of 12, 21 or 40-year-old whisky, it is their legacy we are drinking. But such a legacy is ephemeral, as 'their' spirit evaporates as it matures or is consumed as time passes. Happily, their successors are equally diligent in providing whisky for us to drink in years to come. But what of the stories of those figures who have made a contribution to whisky history at various levels, often through times of dramatically changing fortunes?

Surely the tales they have to tell are worth preserving as a series of still points in the moving heritage of the Scotch whisky industry? So here is my modest attempt to collect, interpret and present a representative selection of them. The intention is to embrace a wide sweep of Scotland's geography and culture, as well as a broad diversity of roles, from maltman and mashman to scientific guru and distillery owner.

As JM Barrie wrote, 'God gave us memory so that we might have roses in December.'

Gavin D. Smith
Denholm Hall
Roxburghshire
March 2013

INTRODUCTION

AS WE SHALL SEE IN the pages ahead, the Scotch whisky industry never stands still. Like all realms of commercial activity it is subject to external pressures, both economic and social, and is therefore prone to periods of 'boom' and of 'bust,' as key markets suffer recessions and growth or drinking fashions change.

What makes the production and selling of Scotch whisky a particularly challenging enterprise is the lengthy period between those two activities. Process cheese or tin baked beans and your product may be on the shelves of retailers in a matter of days, but distil whisky and by law it must sit in a warehouse somewhere in Scotland for a minimum of three years before it can be converted into cash. In many cases, of course, it sits there for many more years, all the time losing volume due to evaporation – the fabled 'angels' share.' So not only do you get no return on the result of your investment and labour for several years, but at the end there will be less of it than you started with!

Given the lengthy lead times between distillation and consumption, it takes an exceptional crystal ball to predict what economic and social factors will prevail three, five, 10, 12 or more years down the line. Consequently, matching output to demand has always been fraught with difficulty, and periods of plenty when sales have been strong have always been followed by a glut of spirit, as demand wanes. So, historically, spurts of new distillery construction and the expansion of existing plants have been followed by distillery closures, both temporary and permanent.

This boom-and-bust cycle was most clearly seen during the late-Victorian period, when spectacular growth, which came on the back of the development of blended whisky and its global success, ended in dramatic recession, with personal fortunes and entire companies being lost in the process.

But this is no mere historical phenomenon. In the lifetimes of all the figures featured in this book, the Scotch whisky industry has seen postwar boom followed by bust in the early 1980s, as international demand for Scotch fell and the level of what the press dubbed the 'whisky loch' rose to a concerning level. Although most of the people interviewed in these pages were focused on life and work in quite a localised way, the product they were making has been strongly influenced by export sales for well over a century.

Cutbacks in production and distillery closures were the order of the day in the early 1980s, as the Scotch whisky industry sought to balance future demand with stock holdings. Most eye-catchingly, the mighty Distillers Company Ltd closed no fewer than 21 of its malt distilleries during 1983 and 1985 and in total 55 Scotch whisky distilleries shut down between 1980 and 2002.

Part of the problem was that although Scotch whisky was an important export commodity, there was great reliance on a small number of key markets, principally North America and several European countries, led by France and Italy. When the US economy began to falter during the second half of the 1970s and drinkers also began to favour wine and white spirits, the effect on the Scotch whisky industry was severe.

Today, we are unquestionably in the middle of another period of boom, with the Distillers' Company Ltd's successor organisation Diageo plc pouring large sums of money into its Scotch whisky infrastructure. Having spent some £40 million creating the vast Roseisle Distillery on Speyside during 2008/9, Diageo is now investing a further £1bn over five years in Scotch whisky production, with plans to build one or even two new 10 million litre-capacity distilleries, expand existing plants and warehousing complexes, and develop more renewable energy facilities. Such expansion would increase total production capacity by as much as 40%, and comes in response to sustained global growth across several key brands, most notably the Johnnie Walker 'family' of blends.

Meanwhile, Pernod Ricard subsidiary Chivas Brothers – Diageo's chief rival in many blended Scotch export markets – is also investing heavily in increasing capacity at existing malt distilleries and intends to build an entirely new one on the site of the old Imperial Distillery at Carron, beside the River Spey.

Most other Scotch whisky distillers have also increased malt spirit capacity where possible, and supplies of grain spirit for blending have been augmented too. Diageo has expanded the capacity of its Cameronbridge grain distillery in Fife from 66 million litres of spirit per annum during 1997, to around 105 million litres in 2013.

The principal reason for so much long-term confidence and such large-scale investment is that the major players in the Scotch whisky industry believe that this time around, the good times really will last. Boom will not fall prey to bust anytime soon. Some of this confidence comes from the sheer diversity of global markets for Scotch today.

Scotch sells in more than 200 countries, and emerging middle-class consumers across Africa, Asia and South America mean that these continents now vie with traditional North American and European territories in terms of importance. The USA and France remain the largest export markets, but in 2011 the 'top 10' also included South Africa, Taiwan, South Korea and Venezuela, and in Brazil Scotch whisky imports rose by 48% in one year.

Overall, according to the Scotch Whisky Association, the total impact of Scotch whisky on Scotland's economy is £4.2 billion – £2.9 billion from the industry itself and £1.3 billion through the industry's supply chain. It supports around 36,000 jobs, both directly and indirectly, and productivity has accelerated to £275,000 per annum for each industry employee. In fact, Scotch whisky outperforms most other industries, with employees adding 57% more value per head than workers in the City of London. Scotch represents almost 4% of the Scottish economy – approximately a quarter of Scotland's exports and also a quarter of the UK's food and drink exports.

Despite the amount of media coverage they generate, single malts still only account for some 10% of all Scotch whisky sales, though in terms of value that figure can be virtually doubled. It is in relation to single malts that a burgeoning micro-distilling movement has begun to emerge, to a more modest extent copying that which now prevails in the USA.

At the time of writing, a new distillery by the name of Wolfburn came on stream in January 2013 at Thurso in Caithness, while the old Annandale Distillery in south-west Scotland is in the process of being rebuilt and re-commissioned after more than nine decades of silence.

Work on creating Kingsbarns Distillery in Fife around an old farm steading is expected to begin later this year while the proprietors of the independent bottlers Adelphi have advanced plans in place for a distillery on the Ardnamurchan peninsula.

All of these ventures are predicated upon sales of a high quality, boutique single malt brand, and provide a real contrast with 'super distilleries' like Diageo's Roseisle. In an industry where so much activity has become concentrated in so few hands, this modest flowering of diversity and independence is surely a welcome development. In 2012, 98 malt whisky distilleries and seven grain distilleries were operational, with Diageo owning 28 of those malt distilleries, while Pernod Ricard held another dozen.

As I wrote at the beginning of this introduction, the Scotch whisky industry never stands still. Since conducting the interviews which form the basis of this book during 2011 and 2012, there have inevitably been some relevant changes, notably the impending sale of Loch Lomond Distillery to a business consortium in the spring of 2013, and the decision by Fred and Stewart Laing to split their bottling business and operate independently of each other.

No doubt by the time you read this, the world of Scotch whisky will have moved on some more, but that is partly what makes it so endlessly fascinating.

PART ONE
Making It

CHAPTER 1
Norman Morrison – Distillery Worker, Talisker

THE ISLE OF SKYE IS ONE of the most dramatically beautiful islands of the Hebrides, with its rugged mountain ranges and plethora of sea lochs slicing into the landscape. It is the largest and most northerly of the Inner Hebrides, with a population of just over 9,000, though this stood at over 23,000 in 1841, before depopulation took its toll during the rest of that century and more.

In Scotch whisky circles Skye is forever associated with Talisker single malt, made in the island's only (legal) distillery. Since the opening of the Skye Bridge in 1995 it has no longer been necessary to travel 'over the sea to Skye,' as the old song puts it, but the island still has a remote feel to it, and while much of the commercial and social life of the island focuses on the 'capital' of Portree, Talisker Distillery is situated some 20 miles to the south-west, and its location is truly remote.

Arguably boasting one of the most striking settings of any Scottish distillery, Talisker stands at the end of the main – and only – street in the small village of Carbost, at the head of Loch Harport, close to the southern end of the Trotternish peninsula, and in the shadow of the famous Cuillin Hills. The placenames of Skye reflect the island's rich, Gaelic heritage, with Portree translating as 'the king's port,' while Carbost is derived from the Gaelic for copse. Talisker itself means 'sloping rock.'

Talisker Distillery dates back to 1830 when brothers Hugh and Kenneth MacAskill leased a site and constructed the distillery. Ultimately, Talisker passed into the hands of the Distillers Company Ltd (DCL) in 1925, and today it is owned by DCL's successor company Diageo, the world's largest distiller. In addition to Talisker, Diageo owns no fewer than 28 operational malt distilleries in Scotland, though the Skye Distillery produces a very distinctive style of whisky, which is highly prized both for blending purposes and by connoisseurs of single malt. After Cardhu, Talisker is Diageo's bestselling single malt.

The powerful, peppery and peaty Talisker is sometimes referred to as 'The lava of the Cuillins,' and the author Robert Louis Stevenson was a fan, writing in 1880 'The king o'drinks as I conceive it, Talisker, Isla or Glenlivet' (*The Scotsman's Return from Abroad*).

One man who has spent much of his life living in close proximity to Talisker Distillery is Norman Morrison, who was born at Portnalong, three miles away. He worked for 28 years after a period of exile, so common to Scottish islanders.

'Most of the people in Portnalong came from Lewis and Harris, in the Outer Hebrides,' he explains. 'Crofts were allocated in the Portnalong area to alleviate overcrowding in Lewis and Harris, and people came over in 1928. Before that there were only two families at Portnalong. When I was a lad, Carbost had two shops, and walking the three miles to Carbost from Portnalong was like going into town. The shops had sweets in after the war!'

Just as the railway network played a major part in supplying many mainland distilleries with the raw materials of whisky-making and transporting away casks of spirit, so island distilleries such as Talisker relied on the sea for the same purpose. Central to the sea-borne servicing of island communities was the 'puffer' – a small cargo ship, often operating out of the River Clyde. Today, Talisker's needs are serviced by road transport, but Norman remembers that when he was a youngster 'There would be as many as five puffers at the Carbost pier at any one time – bringing in coke, empty barrels, barley, one maybe loading up with full casks – there were lots of local people getting employment from that.

'Dutch ships brought in barley from King's Lynn in Norfolk, and I can remember almost all of the names of the puffers that used to come in even now. A company from Glasgow had boats which were all named after African tribes, so you had *Zulu* and such like. Ross and Marshall boats all had 'Light' in their names, *Raylight* and *Starlight* and *Moonlight*.'

With the sea providing most of the distillery's transport needs, the roads around Talisker were decidedly primitive. 'Cinders from the coal-fired stills and the boiler were spread onto the unmade roads all around the distillery area,' he says. 'There was no Tarmac on them, and the council took the ash in a lorry and spread it on the roads. 'Many distillery workers supplemented their incomes by farming a croft, and Norman recalls that, 'Most crofts had two head of cattle for the milk. Bags of draff [*the spent grist left in the mashtun after mashing is completed*] from the distillery would be delivered to the crofts. It was good feed for bringing cattle on for milk. Some went to the farms too, and some went away for animal feed. The rest was dumped in the river, and there were always lots of ducks around it.

'There were sixty-eight crofts in Portnalong when I was a boy, and only very few now. The people who worked in the distillery each had some cattle. They had a steady wage, which meant you could run a croft well. You could build sheds and have decent fencing, and so on. You could tell who was working in the distillery by the state of the crofts!'

Inevitably, entertainment tended to be of the make-your-own variety, though Norman explains that, 'Every second Friday the Highlands and Islands Development Board's mobile cinema came to the old school in Carbost. Ten o'clock at night, after the pictures, we would call into the distillery as lads, and if the man, who was also called Morrison, like me, was away from the malting floor we would play among the bed of malt, we would just run around all over the place. We would go jumping into the barley pits – it's a wonder we weren't suffocated. There would be all these beautiful couches [layers of grain] on the floor, all ploughed and looking lovely, and we would make a right mess of them.

'When I was doing the job years later I recalled what we had done as lads – we had made double the work for the poor man. I used to think if it had been me I'd have murdered the kids! Also, there were two railway lines down to the pier, and they had bogies on them – flat one for barrels and ones with sides for coal. There was a slight incline, and as boys we would ride them down to the pier.'

If the sea served as a vital means of communication for island communities, it also often provided a means of employment for islanders, for whom there was usually little prospect of work at home. 'When you left school you headed for the mainland,' declares Norman, 'and the Merchant Navy was booming when I was young, and lots of the lads from Skye joined that. Every ship had half-a-dozen crew members from the Western Isles on it.'

While away from his native isle, earning a living from the sea, Norman met and married a woman from Teesside, in north-east England, and on leaving the Merchant Navy he secured a job with one of the area's largest employers, the chemical giant Imperial Chemical Industries (ICI).

'I was with ICI for five years and then my brother, who worked at Talisker, told me there was a job going at the distillery. We came up on holiday and my wife liked the place, so I took the job and we got a company house, the same house I'm living in till this day. I started at the distillery in 1972.'

Norman's initial role was as a maltman, working at a time when every malt distillery in Scotland had its own floor maltings. As part of the DCL's programme of distillery expansion and malting centralisation on-site malting ceased at Talisker during 1972, and since then malt has been made to Talisker's specification at Glen Ord Maltings in Inverness-shire. Phenol levels of peating are measured in parts per million (ppm), with many distilleries using malt peated to just one or two ppm, while the most heavily peated Islays will use malt with a phenolic level in excess of 50ppm. Talisker uses a medium-peated malt of 20-22ppm.

The role of maltman was one of the most physically demanding of all distillery roles, and maltmen sometimes suffered from a condition known as bursitis, commonly nicknamed 'monkey shoulder' or 'monkey grips,' due to repeatedly turning the germinating barley, or piece, on the malting floor using wooden shiels, or shovels, in order to prevent the tangling or rootlets and to maintain an even temperature.

Recalling his days as a Talisker maltman, Norman explains that, 'We had two malt barns, with two floors in each. You would have twenty-odd tons in each couch. In summer, if it was humid and foggy, I detested night shift. The barley would sprout like mad, it would just go haywire in that sort of weather, so you had to turn it a lot to stop the rootlets getting tangled. You were on your own from ten pm to six am and you never had much time to yourself. I've never worked so hard in my life. When you went home in the morning, you slept. You certainly didn't need a sleeping pill!

'It was very eerie in the malt barns when you were in there by yourself at night. On a Saturday night I might be the only one working in the barns, and there were rats all over the place. You would sit down for a cup of tea and a 'piece' at maybe two am. One night I was sitting there drinking my tea and eating my piece when suddenly between the two couches of barley a Lurpak butter wrapper appeared – and it was a still night, there was no wind to blow it. It came towards me, and I realised that it was a rat with this butter wrapper in its mouth – it must have got it out of the manager's bin. If I'd had a drink on me I'd have sobered up quickly, I can tell you! I remember I was working in the malt barns when they landed on the moon ... '

Although work in the maltings was hard, there were many lighter moments to compensate for the labour involved. Norman recalls that, 'Roddy Alec was one of the great characters in the distillery. He liked his dram. He wore a pair of thick glasses, and every lunchtime he headed up the road from the distillery to the Old Inn for a pint or two on his break.

'There were no cattle grids around the distillery then and so you would often get sheep in the distillery eating the draff. One day, Roddy Alec came back from the pub and into the maltings where the bags of 'cummins' [dried malt rootlets] were stored. I was following Roddy Alec and I saw that there was a Blackface sheep between two bags. All you could see was the head. Well, Roddy Alec looked and he took off his glasses, and he put them on again and the sheep's head was still there. So he took them off again, rubbed them on his sleeve, put them on again, and still he could see the sheep's head. I was just standing behind him laughing quietly to myself.'

Draff was an important by-product of distilling for the local crofters, for whom it provided valuable animal feed. 'Once a week crofters came up with bags to be filled with draff and they were then delivered by a local guy with a lorry,' says Norman. 'Sometimes, people at the distillery used to put one of the forty-five-pound weights meant to hold down the wooden lids of the washbacks in the tunroom during fermentation into a draff bag for a joke. The lorry driver really used to struggle with them!

'One of the stillmen in my time, Bill Campbell, filled two bags of draff each week and took them away home in the boot of his car after finishing night shift. I used to put weights in them and watch him struggle to get them into the car. He told me that eventually he had about a dozen of the things, and the distillery started to wonder where they had all gone to!'

In common with all island distilleries, peat-harvesting was an important task to be accomplished at Talisker, with the objective being to cut, dry and gather in sufficient supplies of peat to last for a working year. 'In the summer the distillery shut for two months and everybody cut peats for the malting,' recalls Norman. 'They took on extra people to help with the cutting, too. You did it for your own crofts as well as for the distillery. There was a big peat shed near the pier for the distillery. You had a coke fire in the kiln in the maltings, and you had to put so many peats on top of that. The smoke came off from it and flavoured the malt. You had to be careful not to put too much peat on or you could put the fire out.'

> *Malting – Essentially, the purpose of malting is to 'modify' the barley corn by enzymic action, breaking down cell walls and converting the insoluble starch to soluble starch, which will be turned into fermentable sugars during the 'mashing' stage of whisky production. In distillery-based floor maltings, barley is steeped in water for two or three days, then spread on a malting floor, where rootlets develop as germination begins. So that the malt retains the sugars essential for fermentation, germination must be halted at this point, and the partially germinated 'green malt', as it is known, is transferred to a kiln for around seven days and dried over a fire or by jets of hot air, often with some peat used in the furnace to impart flavour. The amount of peat introduced during kilning has a major influence on the character of the finished whisky.*
>
> *Mashing – During the process of mashing, malt is mixed with hot water to form wort. Mashing follows malting and pre-*

cedes fermentation in the whisky-making process, and the mash of grist and hot water is mixed in a large, circular vessel, known as a mashtun. Mashing extracts soluble sugars from the malted grain.

Fermentation – Along with mashing, fermentation is part of the 'brewing' process of whisky production, and a distillery 'mashman' is traditionally responsible for all brewing practices. During fermentation, yeast is added to the wort in a number of wooden or stainless steel washbacks, housed in the 'tunroom,' and the yeast acts upon sugars contained in the wort to produce a low-alcohol beer called 'wash'. This is the first time during whisky-making that alcohol is produced.

After working in the malt barns for two years, Norman followed the usual route of advancement into the mash house when one of the serving mashmen retired. 'It was nothing like such hard work as the maltings,' he notes. 'The old mashtun had rakes in it, and we got good extraction from it. You put the 'stirrer' on as much as you could when you were mashing, and left it on till you had finished. That gave better extraction, better results. The old manager, Hogg, explained that to me.'

A new 'lauter' mashtun was installed in 1997, replacing the existing cast-iron vessel, though unusually it retains a copper dome. Its increased efficiency meant that the mashing cycle was halved from ten to five hours. 'It's made from stainless steel now, and all cleaned with sprinklers,' notes Norman, pointing out that, 'With the old one you had to go inside with a steam hose to clean it, wearing Wellies and an apron and nothing else. I felt great when I came out – it was just like a Turkish bath! I never felt so clean in all my life ...

'The copper dome of the mashtun was polished with Brasso. You had two full shifts every Wednesday doing that, and on reflection, what a waste of manpower that was! Computers came in six months before I left. Now you press a button and it carries out the mashing cycle. Temperatures for mashing were very accurate once computers were put in. Spot on. You could never do that quite so precisely for yourself. Today, you get mentally tired doing the job, but not physically tired.'

Inevitably, the increase in computerisation and the lack of floor maltings, means that the modern Talisker workforce is significantly smaller than it was some years ago. Additionally, whereas at one time spirit was filled into casks and warehoused on site, today the spirit is collected by road tanker and taken away to be casked and matured in central maturation facilities in the central belt of the Scottish mainland, though some is transported back to Talisker for maturation. 'The stills were coal-fired until 1972,' says Norman, 'and you had a mashman, a boilerman and a stillman on shift. There would be eight staff in malt barns during the day, and four on nightshift there. They would also be called on to roll barrels and do other duties from time to time. In the tun room, you had one man just to steam the vats, keeping the washbacks clean, so you are talking 12 men in total per shift.

'Then you had two women in the office, a manager and an under-manager, two excisemen, two drivers for the minibus to collect staff, an electrician, an engineer and coopers, because at that time all the casks were filled and matured on site. All in all, nearly fifty people were employed at the distillery at one time. Today, on a shift you have a mashman and a stillman. There are more tour guides than production staff!'

Modern distilleries are comparatively clean places to work, but in the days when stills were coal-fired it was an entirely different matter. 'The distillery is certainly a lot less dirty than it used to be,' says Norman. 'There was coal dust all over the place. Every Friday night they hosed down the stillroom walls, and you could see the coal dust running down them. But it was great to hear the roar of the fires in the stillhouse, and if you were wet on a winter's night, with gales and rain outside, you put your backside to the still and you could easily get dried there.'

Until the practice cased in the early 1980s, 'dramming' was an essential part of a distillery's routine. This involved the brewer handing out drams of whisky to the staff several times a day, with the size of drams and the frequency of their distribution varying from distillery to distillery. In some cases, new-make spirit was dispensed, and in others, mature whisky.

'We always got stuff from the best cask in the warehouse, not new-make spirit,' notes Norman. 'We were drammed at nine am, twelve o'clock and five pm. The nightshift men coming on got a double dram – a cupful to do them the night. You got an extra dram for cleaning the elevator or similar unpleasant jobs. The postman would always manage to arrive at the distillery at twelve-thirty, just in time for a dram. You didn't need a clock to tell when the post would be delivered!'

Every distillery had its resident excise officer or officers, who represented 'the Crown,' and whose job it was to ensure that no spirit went unaccounted for, in the days before self-policing by distillers was introduced. 'The excise officers were pretty lenient, provided that nobody was abusing the privilege, if you like. There were no accidents that I remember, despite the dramming. The exciseman would come in at two or three in the morning sometimes, you never knew when he would call. He had a great deal of power and had the second-biggest house at Talisker, after the manager.'

Despite dramming, many distillery workers found ingenious ways of liberating spirit for their personal use and that of their friends, but Norman recalls an instance when the liberation of whisky took place far from any distillery.

'Before I was at Talisker, when I was in the Merchant Navy we used to load whisky in Grangemouth, in Fife, and put it off in Rotterdam, en route to the States,' he recalls. 'One night, myself and a fellow from Shetland were coming back from the pictures in Grangemouth when we decided to go into the hold to get ourselves a couple of bottles of whisky. The night watchman was a Skye man and we told him what we were doing and he didn't mind. We pulled out some nails and opened up a case and it was full of miniatures of Old Smuggler. Well we didn't want those, so we had to pack them all pack in and seal up the case.

'We opened up a second case and this time we got the good stuff, Johnnie Walker Black Label. We took out four bottles and replaced them with fire bricks. We did three cases that night, and from then on we did this every trip we made from Grangemouth with whisky. In the States they were convinced it was happening at the bottling plant in Kilmarnock and they were keeping an eye on the workers there!

'Well, many years later when I was working at Talisker there was an excise officer over on relief for three weeks, and he was from Leven in Fife. He came in to chat when I was on the night shift one time and I was telling him about the Merchant Navy, and how I had worked for the Gibson Rankin Line, based in Leith. I told him what we had one with the bottles of Johnnie Walker and he just looked at me in amazement. It turned out he had been based in Leith at the time. 'I was called to London three times over that,' he told me, 'and I've had to come all the way to Skye to find out the truth!'

As a single malt, Talisker is highly prized by owners Diageo, and the 10-year-old expression was one of the six core 'Classic Malts' launched in 1988, the same year a visitor centre opened at the Skye distillery. Today, the range has been extended to include Storm, an 18-year-old, a Distiller's Edition (with an Amoroso Sherry finish) and 57 North, which takes its name from the distillery's latitude and the strength of the whisky.

Norman declares that, 'The whisky I like now is the 18-year-old, it's a nice dram, but I wish I had a bottle of DCL-distilled Talisker, which used to be bottled by Gordon & MacPhail in Elgin. The smell was different to now. You would just think you were at the mashtun. It smelled of the distillery and was beautiful stuff. When they were distilling in the old days they took their time. In fact, if the manager caught you rushing the stills you got into trouble.' Today, with no on-site malting and with spirit tankered away to the mainland to be filled into casks for maturation,

Talisker, like so many distilleries, has effectively lost the beginning and the end of the narrative of malt whisky production.

There is an ongoing debate as to whether there is any discernable difference between single malt whisky matured at its place of production and that matured in vast bonding complexes in the central belt. Norman states that, 'I think it must make a difference if the whisky is matured on the island rather than taken to a central place on the mainland away from the lochs and mountains and so on. Having worked with chemicals at ICI, changes in the chemistry of maturing the whisky in different locations wouldn't surprise me.'

He notes that three of the old, stone warehouses at Talisker have been demolished, and makes the point that, 'When I started work at the distillery only the malt barns were old, with corrugated iron roofs. All the rest was new, having been rebuilt after the fire. It had certainly been very old-fashioned before that.'

The fire in question took place on 22 November 1960, when a valve on the coal-fired number one spirit still was left open during distillation. Spirit escaped from the still and caught fire, resulting in serious damage. The entire stillhouse burned to the ground, but was subsequently rebuilt and equipped with new stills that were exact copies of the originals. The dimensions and configuration of two wash and three spirit stills were faithfully reproduced, and the replacement stills continued to be coal-fired until 1972. The unusual ratio of two wash stills and three spirit stills had its origins in the fact that until 1928, Talisker was triple-distilled, although triple distillation is more usually associated with Lowland distilleries, such as Auchentoshan.

'When I went to work at the distillery the guys never discussed the fire,' says Norman. 'It was due to having open fires and a leaking valve. Nobody would say what really happened, whether it was an error. But I do think that if so much money hadn't been spent rebuilding the distillery in the early 1960s it would probably have closed during the 1980s, when DCL shut so many distilleries. It is more expensive to make whisky on an island than it is on the mainland due to so many extra costs.'

Norman combined his role at Talisker with running a croft, and he notes that, 'I got a croft from my brother when I came to work at the distillery – I was keeping a few Hereford cattle. I actually had two crofts of twenty-six acres each, and when you were doing shift work it fitted in really well with the crofting. I've still got the two crofts today. The Herefords were very docile, good cattle to handle, but after a while I bought six belted Galloways, and I've still got their offspring today. 'When I started at the distillery I got my home free, and I retired when I was just over sixty-three – I got my redundancy money and pension and I was able to buy the house for £25,000. I was lucky to work for DCL and then Diageo. They were good companies to work for. I was at Talisker for twenty-eight years, and I'm seventy-three years old now. I never had a single day off work until the last year I was there, when I had to have a heart operation. I still keep in close contact with everything that's going on down at the distillery, and my son is a stillman – he's worked there for sixteen years.' While many people of Norman's age bemoan the loss of 'the good old days,' and lament changing ways brought by incomers to island communities like Skye, he has no such regrets. 'English people have been coming up and building houses,' he says, 'but not holiday homes, mainly. They have been living here all year round. They have taken more interest in the culture of Skye than the locals do!

'When I look at Carbost now, there only used to be one house on my way up the hill, but now there are a dozen. The roads were done up in the 1950s, and now they're good roads. People would cycle six miles to work on a winter's night before the minibus started up. And if you look at old postcards of the place everything looked like a third-world country. It all looked so bleak. None of the houses were painted white, and they were hard times. It's all improved now.

'If anything broke down on the croft you would have to go to Inverness for welding in the old days. Then some guys came up from Lancashire and started doing welding locally. People are so well off by comparison and the community spirit is better. When you get work it creates independence. When I was in school you'd have patches on your trousers, and people in their seventies don't look old now, the way they used to. The standard of living is much better. I'd hate to go back to the old days!'

CHAPTER 2
Boyo Norquoy – Distillery Worker, Highland Park

IF HEBRIDEAN ISLES SUCH AS SKYE feature placenames of Gaelic derivation then the Orkney and Shetland islands to the north of the Scottish mainland are peppered with locations betraying Scandinavian origins – 'holm' for a haven or safe anchorage, 'wick' or 'goe' for inlet. Such words reflect the Nordic heritage of the islands, which belonged to Norway until the mid-15th century, with as many Norwegian flags as Scottish ones being flown from houses in the principal ports of Kirkwall and Stromness during international football tournaments!

Orkney boasts a wealth of prehistoric treasures, including the Ring of Brodgar, The Standing Stones of Stenness and Maeshowe, while the islands' more recent history is graphically represented by the surviving hulks of ships sunk to form barriers across Scapa Flow in order to protect allied shipping located there during two world wars. So strategically important was Orkney in the Second World War that 60,000 troops were posted into a community of 20,000 residents.

Orkney actually comprises some 70 islands in total, 20 of which are inhabited, and much of the land is very fertile, meaning that agriculture remains an important element in the local economy, along with fishing. The late Orcadian poet and novelist George Mackay Brown – who lived in a house built on the site of the old Stromness Distillery, which closed in 1928 – described Orcadians as essentially ' ... fishermen with ploughs.'

Orkney is also well known for its whisky, with two operational distilleries located within three miles of each other. Scapa Distillery dates from 1885, is owned by Chivas Brothers Ltd and takes its name from the maritime feature beside which it stands, but there is nothing Norse about the name of the more famous of the two whisky-making plants. Highland Park could be situated anywhere in the northern half of Scotland. However, the distillery is one of the oldest in the country, dating from 1798, and is located – appropriately on high ground – just to the south of the island capital of Kirkwall, which over the years has spread out to meet the distillery.

Highland Park was constructed on a site where local church officer Magnus Eunson had previously operated an illicit still, hiding kegs of his whisky beneath the church pulpit, according to local legend! Having been owned from 1895 to 1937 by James Grant, Highland Park was then acquired by Highland Distilleries, and is now in the hands of The Edrington Group, which also has The Macallan single malt and The Famous Grouse and Cutty Sark blends in its portfolio.

Like Talisker from Skye, Highland Park single malt has a unique, though entirely different, 'island' character. Part of Highland Park's distinctive profile is based on the exclusive use of ex-sherry casks for single malt bottlings, while the fact that it remains one of only a handful of distilleries in Scotland which continues to make a percentage of its own malt on traditional floor maltings, is also influential.

The peat used in the Highland Park kilns is notably aromatic, and very different from that employed on the 'whisky island' of Islay. While Islay boasted trees several thousand years ago, and their remains were ultimately incorporated into the island's peat, Orcadian peat is derived from heather, dried grass and plants, as there were no trees on Orkney 3,000 years ago, just as there are very few now, due to the frequent, strong winds that are a feature of the area. Peat is crucial to the prevailing profile of Highland Park, and the distillery owns 2,000 acres of peat land on Hobbister Moor, annually cutting some 200 tonnes to fire the distillery furnace and impart its unique flavour.

Just as maltman and mashman Norman is inextricably linked with his native island of Skye and with Talisker Distillery, so Boyo Norquoy is part and parcel of Orkney and of Highland Park. Principally employed as a stillman until his retirement, his role followed that of mashman in the sequence of malt whisky production.

> *Distillation – This follows the process of fermentation in whisky making. During distillation the alcohol is separated from the wash by heating it in stills. Alcohol boils at a lower temperature than water and is driven off as vapour, leaving behind the water. It is subsequently condensed back into liquid form. Malt Scotch whisky distillation comprises two consecutive distillations in copper pot stills, the first, which takes place in the wash still, produces 'low wines,' which are then re-distilled in the spirit still to produce a stronger spirit, ready to be filled into casks for maturation.*

Born and bred in Kirkwall, 'Boyo' declares that, 'My actual name is Christie, but I've been called Boyo all my life. My sister, who is two years older than me, couldn't pronounce Christie, and she called me Boyo and it stuck. Even the teachers at school called me Boyo.'

The Norse influence that permeates most island place names has also shaped many common Orcadian surnames, such as Isbister, Flett and Norquoy. 'There've been many generations of Norquoys born in the islands, right enough,' confirms Boyo. Just as in Skye, and so many other Scottish island and remote coastal communities, the sea has traditionally offered a means of escape to new horizons and new opportunities, and Orkney has a long heritage of involvement with the Hudson's Bay Company, whose ships regularly stopped over in the islands to take on supplies and recruit labour.

Remarkably, by the late 18th century, three-quarters of the Hudson's Bay Company workforce in Canada were Orcadians. In 1799, of the 530 men working in the Hudson's Bay Company post in North America, no fewer than 416 were from Orkney. 'My father's brother went to Canada around 70 or 80 years ago,' says Boyo Norquoy, 'and I've lots of cousins over in Canada still. Orkney was all about farming and fishing then.'

After school, aged 14, Boyo entered the butchering business and then worked for 17 years in a bacon curer's, followed by a period with the butcher Jonty Flett, until his business closed. 'After that I got a job at Highland Park in 1974,' he says, 'though there were no family distilling connections before I started to work at the distillery. It began with six weeks in the cooperage and warehouses – repairing casks and moving casks full of spirit in and out of the warehouses as required.' The usual progression for workers was from the warehouse squad into the malting operation and then into mashing, but Boyo missed out those 'intermediate' stages. 'One day the brewer asked if I would like a full-time job in the stillhouse,' he notes, 'and I said yes.'

Highland Park is equipped with two pairs of stills, and the distillery can produce up to 2.5 million litres of spirit per year. 'Nowadays the stillhouse is computerised,' observes Boyo. 'The operator just pushes a button to make it work. When I was at the stills you had to control them manually, though they had been converted from coal-firing to oil during the 1960s, as in most distilleries. You would get the wash piped through from the tun room [where fermentation had taken place] and you filled the wash stills with that. You boiled it, got it settled and running nice and cool for gentle spirit. When you were boiling wash you had to make sure you didn't get it boiling over the top. It must be boiling steadily, with vapour going over and condensing. If you drove the still too hard the wash would go over the lyne arm into the condenser.

'The low wines were pumped into the low wines and feints tank, and then you got the low wines stills running. We never ran the stills above ten litres per minute – which was quite a slow speed compared to some other distillers – but it made the spirit much less fiery. If it was fiery when it was new then it would probably still be fiery when it was old! You would run the foreshots for as long as you thought you needed to – and you turned the spirit flow on and off by hand. You had a pride in your job. You worked with temperature and strength – using a hydrometer and thermometer. The strength determined your length of run. You cut when the temperature and strength coincided, according to a chart in the stillhouse.

'You would use controls to regulate the temperature, and you would lower it if there was hot weather, because that would make a difference. The best spirit was made in cold weather; the colder the better. Highland Park has condensers located outside the still house, and the water in them was obviously colder in winter. Then you got a less fiery new make spirit – you could smell the difference.'

When it came to working practices, he notes that, 'You did six am till two pm, two pm till ten pm and night shift in the stillhouse, and then one week in four you were off shift work helping out in the malting and warehouses. That was a lot harder work than the stillhouse!'

However, there was always the traditional reward of a 'dram' by way of compensation. 'One of the big changes in my time in the industry was the end of dramming. You got a dram at lunchtime and at teatime, and the brewer at Highland Park always gave us a good mature dram. I didn't always go for the mature dram because it tended to give me heartburn, but when I drank the clearic or "spike" as it was known, that never gave me heartburn.

'When the distillery was closed during the annual "silent season" for maintenance and so on and there was no new-make to drink, we would go into the filling store, open up the pump that was used to fill casks and empty the spirit out of the sump! The Customs guys thought that if you were drammed you wouldn't take any whisky for yourselves. But this wasn't true, of course!'

Like most distillery workers, Boyo has some colourful tales to tell of the various and ingenious ruses used to 'liberate' whisky. 'One guy was heading home one day from working in the warehouse and the brewer was driving by,' he recalls. 'So he stopped and offered him a lift. The guy said it was okay, he wife was coming to pick him up. Actually, he had two big lemonade bottles of whisky out of the warehouse strapped to his waist and he couldn't sit down!'

Highland Park boasts 23 on-site warehouses, holding some 46,500 casks at any one time. Not surprisingly, these apparently impregnable structures have sometimes been a target for thirsty distillery worker determined to extract an extra dram or two from their employers.

'There used to be some guys who would get up onto the roof of one of the warehouses,' remembers Boyo. 'They would edge open a skylight by pulling back the soft lead around it, put down a pipe and ease out the soft bung from a cask with the end of the pipe. They'd sook the whisky up the pipe and into a tin on the rooftop, then ease the bung back in, put the glass on the skylight back into place, push the soft lead back around it. Nobody ever knew they'd been up there!

'In the cooperages you had "dippers" or "dogs" and you'd pull so much out of a cask, and have a dog in your pocket and a bottle or a half-bottle to fill. You wore a "brattie" – a warehouse cooper's apron that was like a sack – and you made it hang to hide the shape of the bottle.'

At that time, every distillery was allocated at least one resident excise officer, who was charged with accounting for every drop of spirit produced, as it was liable to excise duty, and governments have always been keen to extract as much money as possible from the Scotch whisky industry.

'You were pretty sure the Customs and Excise guys knew what was going on,' says Boyo, 'and the customs man would no doubt have his own drop. But there was no sense of it ever being sold by anyone – it was just for your own consumption.

'We went inside the boilers during the closed season, chipping off hard, burnt oil with a chipping hammer, and you got a "stourie" dram, or a "dirty dram" as it was sometimes known, for doing that, in addition to your usual drams. Sometimes you would get dirt from one of the contractors doing something at the distillery and rub it on your face, and you'd go to the brewer and get a dirty dram by saying it was very hard work – even though you hadn't been doing it!'

Even in the stillhouse it was possible to augment accepted dramming practices, with Boyo noting that, 'We had a wee "pull" of white spirit now and again. You could get it out of the spirit safe. You got a wee tube and you fed it in through a corner of the safe and into the sample jar – you would just sook it out. We would fill small bottles to take away sometimes. And the other guys working on night shift came down and had a dram of it with you.'

Most distillery workers have a favourite 'legal' expression of the whisky that they help to produce, but Boyo says that, 'I always drank new-make or vodka, then when I'd been retired from the distillery for three years I took a job as a lollipop man at the school crossing. I knew everybody, of course, and one day a woman gave me a bottle of Three Barrels brandy as a thank-you for cheering people up each day. I had a dram and didn't get any heartburn. So now I have three or four drams of brandy every night. I find Tesco's own brand in a plastic bottle is good.'

Asked to nominate the principal changes he has seen during his career in the Scotch whisky industry, Boyo singles out the cessation of dramming, and the introduction of computers into the workplace.

'I retired at fifty-eight,' he notes, 'when computers and multi-skilling were coming in. Now the guys do malting, mashing and distillation. I've been retired ten years and I breed fancy pigeons, which I've been doing for more than sixty years.'

Another significant difference that Boyo observes on the whisky scene is the rise to prominence of single malts during the past two or three decades. Today, around 75% of all Highland Park produced is reserved for single-malt bottling rather than for blending, and the extensive range of single malts on offer embraces 12- to 50-year-olds, along with many limited edition and travel retail-exclusive expressions.

'When I started work at Highland Park the only single malt was a ten-year-old,' says Boyo. 'A great deal of it went into the Famous Grouse blend. Then people became aware of single malts and there are a colossal lot of whiskies around now.'

Like Norman Morrison on Skye, Boyo has seen many changes on Orkney during his lifetime, but he is less positive about some of them than his Hebridean counterpart.

'There's been a growth in the amount of housing on Orkney and lots of incomers,' declares Boyo. 'But the population isn't up any. There are 550 people living on the island of Sanday, and only a hundred are Orcadians. You lose tradition and you lose culture. People who move to new places always want to change things. But I always say there are two things they can't change in Kirkwall – the pipe band and 'The Ba'.'

'The Ba' is officially titled 'The Kirkwall Ba' Game' and follows an ancient tradition of such sporting events, which are staged in location from the Northern Isles to the Scottish Borders and beyond. 'The Ba' is one of the highlights of the Kirkwall social calendar, taking place on Christmas Day and New Year's Day, and the mass football match features the rival 'Uppie's and 'Doonies', with up to 200 people battling for their respective teams.

Without Boyo and his contemporaries, Highland Park Distillery is undoubtedly a less entertaining place to work, as he and selected colleagues had a fondness for practical jokes, ' ... to liven up the place a bit.'

'One of the people I worked with was Ian Tulloch,' he recalls. 'Now, there's an intercom in the stillhouse for guides to use during tours, and Ian could imitate a fire alarm very accurately. One day when I was on duty in the stillhouse he came in and did it through the intercom. People appeared from everywhere. It cleared all the buildings! The manager wasn't impressed and said it wasn't his sense of humour. I was shop steward of the union, and despite him shouting I refused to tell him who had done it.

'There's a display of casks in one of the warehouses where guides take visitors to explain to them about the use of ex-sherry casks and so on, and one day a guide was doing this when Ian leaps up from under the last barrel in the row and runs off!'

Another particularly memorable ploy involving Ian Tulloch and Boyo took place one Christmas several years ago. 'The visitor centre was open in the evening,' says Boyo, 'and Ian dressed as an old woman with a tweed coat and skirt and headscarf, while I dressed in old clothes and a cap. We went in and went round the shop complaining loudly about the prices and generally causing a bit of a stir, and we could see in the mirrors all the staff watching and whispering to each other. They had no idea who we were, until finally one of them realised and they threw us out!'

CHAPTER 3
Jim Cryle – The Glenlivet

ONE OF THE MOST FAMOUS NAMES in the world of Scotch whisky is Glenlivet. Not only is The Glenlivet the second-bestselling single malt whisky in the world and the leader in the USA, but the brand and its distillery are at the very heart of Scotch whisky's remarkable heritage.

Glenlivet is a remote and wildly beautiful area of north-east Scotland, within the Speyside region of malt whisky production, where around half of all Scotland's malt distilleries are to be found today. Glenlivet was famous for the quality and abundance of its illicit whisky long before George Smith made history by being the first person in the area to take out a licence in the wake of the influential 1823 Excise Act, which made distilling an altogether more attractive commercial proposition in the Highlands. Indeed, Smith's family had been making whisky on their farm at Upper Drumin in Glenlivet since 1774, so they were not exactly novices at the game.

What George Smith did have to contend with, however, was the hostility of his neighbours, who did not share Smith's enthusiasm for legal distilling. A local landowner, the Laird of Aberlour presented Smith with a pair of hair-trigger pistols with which to protect himself and his distillery, and as Smith later recalled, 'I got together two or three stout fellows for servants, armed them with pistols and let it be known everywhere that I would fight for my place to the last shot.'

The distillery survived and thrived, and in 1840 George Smith leased the Cairngorm Distillery at Delnabo, near Tomintoul and his son, William, took charge of the distillery at Upper Drumin. However, demand for Smith's whisky still outstripped supply, and in 1858 a new, significantly larger distillery named Glenlivet was established on the present Minmore site, with Upper Drumin and Cairngorm closing the following year.

Since 1840 the Edinburgh whisky agency of Andrew Usher & Co had represented Glenlivet in southern Scotland and in England, and in 1864 the firm also undertook to export the whisky. Glenlivet was soon being sold in international markets with notable success.

Today, internationalism continues to be the name of the game, and The

Glenlivet is in the hands of the world's second-largest distiller of Scotch whisky, Pernod Ricard, which operates another dozen Speyside distilleries, under its Chivas Brothers subsidiary, which was acquired from Seagram Distillers Ltd in 2001.

One individual who came to be intimately associated with The Glenlivet Distillery and its single malt during his 44-year career in the Scotch whisky industry was Jim Cryle. Jim was born at Tarland, some 30 miles west of Aberdeen and attended the local primary school and Banchory Academy. 'I then joined the North of Scotland College of Agriculture as a "lab tech",' he says. 'There were no connections with the whisky industry; the family had crofts and farms in the Buchan area of the north-east going back, and on my mother's side, the family were shoemakers.

'While I was working with the college they were doing research on barley for Long John Distilleries, which gave me an interest in the subject, and I had grown up with a farming background, in an area where lots of barley was grown, so I had an interest in grain anyway. I then got a job as assistant manager for the maltings at Tamdhu Distillery. They wanted someone with laboratory experience. I was twenty-one-years-old and they took me on as a management trainee in 1966, with a year being spent in Robertson and Baxter's laboratory in Glasgow, involved in whisky analysis, before I moved to Tamdhu.'

At that time, Tamdhu, located close to the River Spey, was owned by the Highland Distilleries Co Ltd, associated with the Glasgow-based brokers and bottlers Robertson & Baxter Ltd, and it operated Saladin Boxes in the maltings. These were rectangular-section concrete troughs with perforated floors in which barley was steeped and turned by mechanical rakes prior to malting.

Jim recalls that, 'I set up a production control lab and was there for three years, from 1967 until 1970, when I moved to the company's Bunnahabhain Distillery on Islay as Assistant Manager. We loved Islay, and the early seventies was a boom time on the island. All the distilleries were in full production, and it was a very casual, laidback way of life after what I'd been used to. One day Jim noted that, 'bags of malt dressings had been lying in the maltings at Bunnahabhain for months, and so I asked the workers to clear them up. Several hours later I found the workers in question helping out in the filling store. "You didn't say you wanted it done today," one of them said! That was Islay.'

In 1972 Jim was transferred back to the mainland to Glenglassaugh Distillery at Portsoy on the shores of the Moray Firth. 'I was there for two years and during my time at Glenglassaugh we did experimental work, trying to make the spirit closer in character to Glenrothes. It just wasn't right stylistically for the Cutty Sark blend, which was principally what we needed it for.

'We tried taking water from Glenrothes to Glenglassaugh and mashing and distilling with it, and we sent fermented wash to Glenrothes for distillation. These variations all gave us different spirit. We altered the "cut points" when we distilled at Glenglassaugh and finally decided to replace the stills with ones which were identical to those at Glenrothes. That gave us something closer.' Glenglassaugh was ultimately mothballed in 1986, but found a new lease of life under the ownership of the Scaent Group in 2008. 'I'm very pleased to see it up and running again,' he says.

From Glenglassaugh Jim returned to Tamdhu as General Manager, at what was a time of ongoing growth in the Scotch whisky industry. 'In 1974 to 1975 I oversaw the expansion of the distillery. We built a new tunroom and mash house and extended the stillhouse from four to six stills.

'I was there until 1983, when I became involved in marketing Highland Park and Tamdhu single malts. This was the time of the first real growth in single malts and I soon became aware of just what potential there was. They were pushing Tamdhu, but mainly Highland Park, introducing it to The Famous Grouse blend customers. Tamdhu is a lovely, sweet Speyside whisky, but it was just another Speyside, if you like, whereas Highland Park had a unique style and story to it.'

Jim spent eight years in that particular role, but as he says now, 'To be honest, my heart wasn't really in driving a desk and number-crunching. I let it be known in the Scotch whisky industry that I wanted back into production and I was offered the manager's job at The Glenlivet by Chivas Brothers. I started there in January 1991, and that was the crème de la crème for me. It was a very prestigious appointment.'

As Jim puts it, 'The Glenlivet has a wonderful story and an easy one to tell. It's a story not invented by the marketing people, either! It's an accepted fact that the area was a hotbed of illicit distilling going back two hundred years. It was a very inaccessible place, which meant that people like George Smith could take their time to make the very best spirit. They were extremely unlikely to be caught by the gaugers [excise officers] as the glen gave them lots of cover and they would see them coming for miles. As far as Scotch whisky is concerned, time is the master of perfection. Their stuff wasn't rough or fiery, they took the time to take the best "cut" of spirit. It would be drunk mostly without much maturity.

'George Smith set the standard for a style of whisky that was much copied. He was a good businessman, a visionary, and he knew how to make great whisky. Eventually, twenty-five or so distilleries attached

"Glenlivet" to their names.' Rather like Talisker on Skye, Glenlivet Distillery enjoys such a magnificent setting that only remarkably well-designed and sympathetic buildings can do justice to it, and the architects who added to, altered and replaced Smith's 1858 original distillery were employed for their abilities to create the functional rather than the aesthetically pleasing.

'Through the sixties and seventies there was a need to expand, which meant, sadly, that the three pagodas were knocked down. Then the dark grains plant was built to process by-products, so it's not the prettiest distillery. But they have addressed that with the new extension. They've made a really nice job of that.'

The extension in question, dressed in local stone, was constructed during 2008/9, when £10 million was spent increasing potential capacity to 10.5 million litres per year. Chivas Brothers' avowed intention was to knock Glenfiddich off the international 'number one' single malt spot and such a strategy required larger amounts of maturing spirit being available on an ongoing basis. A highly efficient new mashtun was installed in the new production area, along with eight washbacks and six new stills.

'The stills today are the same shape and size as in George Smith's day, which says a lot for him,' declares Jim. 'They've tried to address the fact that additions to the distillery have not been done very authentically over the years. As you drive up to the distillery now, it looks much better. They also decided to put in new wooden washbacks, rather than ones made from stainless steel.

'I was pleased with that, as it maintains tradition, but it also makes a practical difference. You can never totally sterilise the wood. Beneficial bacteria survive the cleaning process. Also, in a stainless steel washback you don't have the same insulation properties and the influence of temperature. Hotter fermentation reduces detrimental bacterial activity. It's not such an acidic fermentation, which leads to a better spirit.' By the time Jim was appointed to The Glenlivet manager's job in 1991, the tradition of each distillery having its own manager living on site was dying out, particularly among large companies such as Chivas Brothers, which owned a number of distilleries in relatively close proximity. 'We also had a central warehousing function and maintenance team because there were so many Chivas distilleries situated in the area,' says Jim. 'We had a semi-automatic facility at Keith, and all spirit was tankered there for filling. There were better communications and you didn't need to be on-site twenty-four hours a day anymore. I bought a house in Aberlour, a dozen miles from the distillery, but in winter you needed to carry snow chains in your car!

'In 1983/84 we got a huge snowfall as late as May. It was always a couple of degrees colder in Glenlivet than it was in Aberlour. You were rough-ly 1,000 feet up. This affected maturation in the warehouses. Cold and damp conditions in stone-built, dunnage warehouses are far and away the best. You get slow maturation, which means you lose fiery elements, not water, as you do with warm and dry conditions.'

Traditional close-knit distilling community values had long been part of The Glenlivet dynamic, thanks to the distillery's isolated location, but over time this sense of community has diminished. 'There were thirty-odd houses, all occupied by distillery employees but gradually the distillery sold them off because younger people all had cars and they didn't want tied houses', says Jim 'Until the sixties, average people couldn't afford cars. Wages went up as demand for whisky increased, and in particular there was lots of overtime being paid. Workers had a good standard of living then and could pay for cars, and they chose to live away.

'There were about eight vacant houses built in the thirties or forties when I was there. They had built some new bungalows and they were still being used by distillery staff. The older houses have now been sold and modernised.

'I think you've inevitably lost the sense of distillery community. The people who have moved into the houses are not familiar with the way of life and with distilling. There's not the same reliance on neighbours in times of trouble, and people don't need to make their own entertainment. In the fifties, the distillery had about forty staff, but in my time there were only ten production guys working in the distillery, though they took a great pride in 'their' whisky and had a real interest in what it was doing around the world.'

There has long been a close connection between farming and distilling, with whisky-making originally being a way for farmers to add value and longevity to barley crops, while the high-protein draff produced during the mashing process made ideal cattle feed. In turn, the manure produced by those cattle fertilised the fields on which the next crop of barley would grow.

'We had the tenancy of the farm at the distillery until the mid-nineties,' notes Jim, 'with one thousand sheep and a hundred head of cattle, and lots of grazing rights. The land was tenanted from the Crown Estates.

'Cardhu Distillery had a farm, too, and lots of distillers had started as farmers. They were farmers first and distillers second in the old days. The Glenlivet was a farm with a distillery added on originally. Apart from any-thing else, having the land gave you protection of water rights – the lifeblood of the distillery. You could protect it from contamination, for one thing.'

In 1997 Jim took on the role of Master Distiller, and moved into Elgin, where he still lives today. Despite his fondness for hands-on distilling, Jim found that, 'Twenty-five percent of my job at Glenlivet was PR. We got lots of overseas trade customers, and as "Master Distiller" I developed and ran training courses and spent around twenty weeks per year travelling overseas. When Pernod Ricard bought the distillery in 2001 from Seagram they brought more overseas customers to the distillery.'

Embracing his PR role with enthusiasm and a keen eye on the heritage that underpinned The Glenlivet Distillery and the single malt it produced, Jim organised a headline-grabbing event in 1996, when he was one of three people who took a number of ponies, loaded with small casks of Glenlivet on a trek from the distillery. 'We took them over the hills to Tomintoul,' he explains, 'recreating the route George Smith would have taken to get his whisky to market. It was July, but there was ice on top of our tent in the morning! We really appreciated what the old smugglers had gone through. We ended up in the car park of Balmoral Castle, and there we were, a bunch of unshaven guys with a kettle in the place where bewildered tourists arrived by coach to see Queen Victoria's Highland home!'

From that venture, the idea of creating a 'Smugglers' Trail' was born, and out of that evolved short walks through the hills around The Glenlivet Distillery for visitors to take, and, more recently, a series of trails in association with Crown Estates was established.

'Alan Greig, who was in charge of the company's PR, also had the idea of getting a little still and setting it up so that people just came across it while on their trail,' says Jim. 'So I found two model stills in storage at our Strathisla Distillery, and they had very thick tops and boil balls, but no bottoms. I took one and got a coppersmith to weld a base into it and add a copper coil inside half a barrel, making a condensing 'worm.' It made very good whisky – you could distil it nice and slow. It makes a real Glenlivet style, sweet and rich as new-make spirit. We had a fifty-litre ex-Bourbon cask and a fifty-litre ex-sherry cask filled, and they are coming up three years old soon, so it will be interesting to see how it matures.'

The still itself is below the minimum legal capacity usually allowed, so, as Jim explains, 'We had to get special permission from Customs and Excise to use it. The 'sma' still' as we call it can only be used in the distillery environs; we weren't allowed to take it up on the hill and operate it as we had hoped. We can't sell the whisky, either. But it's real fun and it has captured people's imaginations. We only do the second distillation in it, using wash which has been produced in the distillery and been run through the wash stills. We only run it half-a-dozen times a year, which was one proviso from Customs and Excise.'

When it comes to the more formal output of The Glenlivet, Jim describes the single malt as, 'Relatively sweet-tasting, fruity and floral. There is a deceptive depth of character. It's very smooth and easy to drink at first, and then you get secondary flavours developing after that.'

When Jim first became involved with The Glenlivet the only expressions were a 12-year-old and a 21-year-old. 'This was because the owner at the time, Seagram, was not investing behind the brand as I thought it should. The Glenlivet was the number one single malt in the USA, but the view of young Edgar Bronfman, the company CEO, was just to let it cruise along, mainly in US markets. He really wanted to be a movie mogul anyway! It was only when Pernod Ricard took over in 2001 that things really started to happen.

'Twenty-one-year-old The Glenlivet Archive was introduced in my time, but it wasn't until Pernod took over that it was developed in a global sense, and the annual release of a vintage bottling in the Cellar Collection has produced some wonderful whiskies.

'Of the regular line up, the eighteen-year-old is a superb whisky to sip and savour. It's my personal favourite on a Friday or Saturday evening by the fireside. You get a much slower development of flavour than you do with the 21-year-old, which is all up-front. We did a French oak release, too, but decided not to use wine casks – and stay true to George Smith's ideas – so we have just experimented with different non-wine casks, including Limousin oak. We've used very little sherry wood since the fifties, partly because too much sherry influence would mask the delicate flavours of the whisky in a way ex-Bourbon, American oak doesn't.'

Inevitably, during a career in the Scotch whisky industry spanning more than four decades, Jim has seen many changes, starting with the very beginning of the whisky-making process. 'Barley was not malted at individual distilleries any more from the early to mid-sixties,' he notes. 'You get a better, more consistent product from centralised maltings. However, closing distillery maltings had an impact on distilling communities because in each case you lost eight to ten jobs as a result.

'From the late sixties up to the very early eighties you saw lots of distillery expansion. In many cases, there was a doubling of capacity, and there was the introduction of more and more automated systems. Automation of the mashing process was the first to be done. You got automatic temperature control and a timed "run off". It was a big thing at the time. Then you got the remote control of pumps, valves and motors. All centralised on one control panel. More recently came the automatic control of stills, and their "cut points". It's only in the last ten years or so that you've had equipment to monitor the strength of spirit flow from the stills.'

He also points out that, 'Energy conservation has become very important. Energy became the second-largest production cost after the purchase
of barley. Seventy percent of costs was barley and fifteen to twenty percent
was energy. Now you have things like heat recovery and the re-use of hot
water from the condensers. For a time some distillers went in for operations like growing tomatoes, which they did at Glengarioch in
Aberdeenshire and others farmed fish, including eels. John Grant at
Glenfarclas even tried crayfish. Unfortunately, nobody told him they were
cannibals and he ended up with one bloody big crayfish! It was a bit of a
case of the tail wagging the dog, so mostly these stopped.'

Another significant change within distilleries has been the removal of
excise officers. 'When I started working in distilleries you had one resident
excise officer and two assistants, or "watchers". You had to get the excise
officer to unlock the spirit safe if there was a blockage, for example. That
sort of thing made life harder for distillery managers. It was the same with
warehouses. There always had to be the exciseman and the manager
together when one had to be opened up. They both had keys which were
needed to unlock the place. The advent of "self-policing" in the eighties,
when resident excise officers disappeared, made life much easier.'

Unlike some of his contemporaries who mourn the 'good old days', Jim
feels that most changes within the Scotch whisky industry have been for
the best. 'Whisky is much better made than in the old days,' he says,
unequivocally. 'For me, quality equals consistency – modern monitoring
and control make that possible. The guys on night shift in the stillhouse
might have had "one too many" in the past! Also, we are much more aware
of the importance of good wood now. Overall, we have a more consistent
product today.'

He notes that, 'As Master Distiller I've seen lots of parts of the world
and I like to think I've done my bit to help sales and awareness of The
Glenlivet. It's been reinvigorated in the States and there has been big
growth in China, as well as some European markets. It's been very pleasing to see how the brand has grown with the investment put behind it by
Pernod Ricard.

'During the nineties the importance of brand ambassadors was recognised. There is now a huge interest in Scotch whisky around the world,
and long may it continue. The trend of drinking it has finally got away
from an insistence on not putting anything in your whisky, and companies
now encourage people to drink it the way they want to. I used The
Glenlivet brand as an example, if you like, of all that was best about Scotch
whisky. I saw my role as being an ambassador for the drink and also for
Scotland.'

CHAPTER 4
Gordon Dey – Dallas Dhu

JUST AS THE ENTERTAINMENT WORLD describes an unused theatre as 'dark,' so an unused distillery is said to be 'silent.' And for the whisky lover, the saddest sight of all is a 'silent' distillery. No bustle of human activity, no aromas of mashing or of maturing spirit. It is a place of true silence.

Given that Scotch whisky must age for a legal minimum of three years before it may be referred to as such, and in practice is often kept for much longer before being blended or bottled as single malt, it takes a particularly effective crystal ball to accurately match current production to future sales, perhaps a dozen years down the line.

Thus, the Scotch whisky industry has always been prone to periods of 'boom' and 'bust.' Years of buoyant trading lead to the construction of new distilleries and the expansion and modernisation of existing ones, but then sales begin to taper away for various economic and social reasons, yet because of the 'time lag' between production and consumption, surplus stocks of maturing whisky build up, their value falls, and the ultimate result of such over-production is distillery closures.

There have been two such major 'boom and bust' eras, the first during the latter years of the 19th century, when so many of the distilleries we see scattered across the Scottish landscape today were built during 'boom,' and the years around the turn of the century, when the house of cards caused by a glut of whisky came tumbling down during 'bust.'

The second such period came in the early 1980s, following dramatic programmes of expansion during the sixties and seventies in particular. The press dubbed the surplus the 'whisky loch', giving a Scottish twist to the familiar 'wine lake' and 'butter mountain' that created such opprobrium for the European Economic Community (EEC), as it was then styled.

Industry leader DCL responded to the situation by closing no fewer than 21 malt distilleries during 1983 and 1985, and the company's workforce was cut by 470. Whereas there had been 123 operational distilleries in Scotland in 1979, that figure had fallen to 94 a decade later.

Statistics are ultimately just statistics, but for each individual distillery that closes, there is a story of human loss to tell as well. One man who was intimately involved with one of the DCL distilleries that closed in 1983 was Gordon Dey, then working at Dallas Dhu Distillery, near Forres, on Speyside.

Dallas Dhu had been born out of the late-Victorian whisky boom that saw no fewer than 21 new distilleries constructed on Speyside during the last decade of the 19th century alone. Blended Scotch whisky was becoming a drink for the world by this time, and blenders found the comparatively subtle, urbane single malts of Strathspey ideally suited for their purposes. Dallas Dhu was designed by that doyen of 'whisky architects' Charles Doig of Elgin, being constructed during 1898/99. Production commenced in April 1899, and the following year the distillery was sold by its founder, local landowner and distilling entrepreneur Alexander Edward, to the Glasgow blending firm of Wright & Greig Ltd, principally to provide supplies of malt spirit for their Roderick Dhu blend.

The young Gordon Dey entered the Scotch whisky industry some six decades after Dallas Dhu came on stream, initially joining DCL in 1966, aged 16. 'I was born at Rothiemay, north of Huntly, in rural Aberdeenshire and there was no heritage of distilling in the family,' he recalls. 'My father and two brothers were in farming, and the brothers run the farm now. I left school at fifteen and I didn't want to be a farmer, I wanted to make my own way, if you like.'

Gordon's 'local' distillery was Knockdhu, which, like Dallas Dhu was a product of the 1890s Speyside whisky bonanza, and was actually the first distillery to be built – during 1893/94 – by the DCL. 'I started working in the malt barns at Knockdhu Distillery in 1966,' says Gordon, 'but I was there for less than a year, as owners DCL were closing down individual distillery floor maltings at the time and building new, centralised and mechanised malting plants, like that at Burghead, near Elgin.'

Having left Knockdhu after a relatively brief introduction to the Scotch whisky industry, Gordon undertook agricultural and forestry work, before getting married. 'Then one day I saw an advert for a tunroom man at Dalwhinnie Distillery,' he says. 'I was a young guy of twenty, and I'd never been south of Aviemore. When I got there it was raining and misty and the place seemed really bleak, and I thought 'Do I really want to have this job?' but I went through with my interview anyway. And, of course, they offered me the job. Well, I decided to take it, but I made sure I arrived with my wife in the dark!'

Dalwhinnie is yet another 1890s distillery, and enjoys a dramatic and beautiful setting, close to the A9 Perth to Inverness trunk road, though at over 1,000 feet above sea level, and some 13 miles from the nearest town, it can be a daunting place in winter. 'We moved there in November 1970,' notes Gordon, 'and it was a grand place to work, though very antiquated at the time. I remember we would collect the milk from the "milk train" and deliver it to all the distillery houses. We spent two years there and I enjoyed the work, but my wife didn't like Dalwhinnie, it was really just too remote.

'In order to get a move within DCL I had to take a job as a labourer initially, but it was at Dallas Dhu Distillery, near Forres, which was much more to my wife's liking. It's in a lovely situation and was much closer to friends and family. We went there in November 1972. The distillery was a lot smaller and more compact than Dalwhinnie, and while the boiler at Dalwhinnie was still coal-fired, that at Dallas Dhu was running on heavy fuel oil.

'We lived in one of the distillery houses and brought up our two daughters there. They were very young at the time. It was a great community, and everyone helped each other. In the distillery there were eight shift workers, a mill man and three guys in the warehouses.'

Gordon's initial job was as relief mashman, standing in for a mashman who was on holiday at the time, but when he returned to his post, he found himself acting as labourer for a while, before being appointed to the position of millman, responsible for ensuring that the malt was ground into grist, with just the right proportions of flour and husk to ensure optimum fermentation. He recalls that, 'I then became a mashman again, spent time as a stillman and finally started to train as a brewer.'

The 'brewer' in a distillery acted as what would now be termed a production manager, being responsible for day to day running of the distillery on a practical level, and answerable to the distillery manager. One crucial role undertaken by the brewer was 'dramming'.

'Dramming stopped when I was at Dallas Dhu,' remembers Gordon. 'We always got a mature dram. The brewer and the warehousemen knew the best casks to take. We were getting excellent whisky. But guys were driving home from work when they shouldn't really have been driving, so it was as well it stopped I suppose.

'Mature spirit lingered longer on you. New spirit gave you a buzz then left quicker. Heavy manual labour at the time meant that you sweated it off anyway. "Dirty drams", awarded for undertaking sometimes unpleasant tasks outside the usual routine, meant that you never had any trouble getting guys to do anything!'

Dallas Dhu had always operated just one pair of stills, and had a perennial problem with its water supply, which dried up entirely during the infamous drought of 1976. Despite the fact that owners DCL did invest in the site, increasing capacity by installing an additional pair of washbacks in

1964, along with a new mashtun and boiler, subsequently replacing the stills and then converting them to steam-heating, but Dallas Dhu's coat was always hanging on a shooglie peg, to use the Scots vernacular.

As Gordon says, despite the upgrading work that had been done, 'Dallas Dhu was still old-fashioned and small. Aultmore and Linkwood and lots of other DCL distilleries were being rebuilt and extended during the early seventies, but Dallas Dhu was making only between forty and fifty hogsheads of spirit per week. You would be filling that in a day at some of the bigger distilleries, and Teaninich, where I went after Dallas Dhu, would be filling up to ten times as much spirit.'

The distillery had endured a period of silence between 1930 and 1936, as DCL – who had acquired the site in 1928 – tried to curb over-production in the Scotch whisky industry by buying up and closing a significant number of distilleries. Sadly, silence was again to descend on the small distilling community in 1983.

'We knew by the early eighties that there was too much whisky being made,' says Gordon. 'There wasn't so much mature spirit going out and the warehouses were really filling up. We became aware that something must happen. You always found out a lot about what was happening from the lorry drivers who visited the distillery. They were usually pretty well informed because they went to so many places and heard so much.

'We were told in early 1983 that Dallas Dhu was to close, that it wasn't cost effective. A small distillery like that was not so viable. We knew we would be one of the ones to go. Overall, the closures had quite a big effect on Speyside.

'We did a four-day week there for a while, and to be fair, they tried to keep the distillery open for as long as it could. The closures were all about cost. If a distillery produced a light blending whisky then the blender could work without that particular malt as quite a number of distilleries produced a light spirit.

'So it wasn't surprising that those distilleries went. But it was sad to see the industry losing distilleries, jobs and whole distilling communities. It was a particularly sad day when we filled the last cask on sixteenth of March 1983. My name is one of those written on the wall in the filling store as one of the people present, preserved for visitors to see now.'

The distillery was duly mothballed, with Gordon describing the process of shutting down a distillery, yet ensuring it would be in the best possible condition to be re-commissioned should circumstances change. 'We internally cleaned the malt bins, malt conveyors and the grist bin. The insides of the sparge tank and warm water tank were cleaned, washed out and given a coating of lime. This was done to kill bacteria that might still be lingering in any porous area. Hot lime was made into a solution and brushed onto the internal walls of the tanks.

'The inside of the mashtun was cleaned and the plates lifted, and a coating of sperm oil was painted onto the sides and floor. This was to save the cast iron from rusting, but realistically it would have needed to be done periodically over the last thirty years to do any good. The washbacks were filled with water and all pipework cleaned. The stills were cleaned internally as was the boiler. The boiler smoke tubes were cleaned and oiled and the faceplates painted with red oxide paint. The intermediate spirit receiver was filled with water, as were the wooden washbacks to prevent the wood from shrinking, leading to leakage. Engineers were also brought in to decommission some of the machinery.

'Three employees were kept on to wind-up the warehouses, and all the others were made redundant, apart from me. We all hoped that it would open again, but we knew in our hearts that it would not happen.'

Unlike so many of its fellow distilleries which closed during the eighties and were subsequently demolished or converted for other uses, Dallas Dhu did at least survive intact, and now has a valuable interpretive role for visitors. It was leased by DCL to the organisation that is now Historic Scotland to be preserved and opened to the public, and the fact that it was compact, complete and relatively original, made it an ideal selection for the role. The old distillery re-opened as a visitor attraction in 1988. 'I would love Historic Scotland to come along and ask me to get it going again,' says Gordon with a wistful smile. 'That would be fantastic!'

Just as Gordon's initial foray into the distilling business at Knockdhu had been followed by time out of the industry, so it seemed that a similar fate would befall him when Dallas Dhu closed. 'I was due to go to work in the milk-bottling factory in Forres,' he says, 'when I was told there were three DCL brewers jobs going, at Talisker on Skye, Brora in Sutherland and Teaninich, at Alness, north of Inverness. We went to Teaninich.'

By contrast with the late-Victorian distilleries of Knockdhu, Dalwhinnie and Dallas Dhu, where Gordon had previously worked, Teaninich had a much longer history, dating back to 1817. However, the original distillery had been augmented in 1970 by a new distillation unit, comprising six stills and known as the 'A' side. This was in line with DCL's policy of expanding existing distilleries during the sixties and early seventies.

'When I went there the new plant had been producing spirit for a number of years, and the old "side" was still working too,' notes Gordon. 'It was all very different to Dallas Dhu. For one thing, the house (that went with the brewer's position) was in Alness, so we were living in a town after living in the country. As this was my first brewer's job, it was a big learning curve for me. Everybody helped everyone else at Dallas Dhu and at Teaninich I found there was something of a "that's not my job" attitude. Indeed, one Saturday, after the last shift of the week had finished, just to help out I went into the stillhouse and cleaned out a still. Come Monday morning, the shop steward was in the manager's office complaining about me. Needless to say I never cleaned another still!'

The 'boom' and 'bust' nature of whisky-making saw the old or 'B' side of Teaninich close down in 1984, and the following year the 'A' side was also mothballed, once again leaving Gordon seeking a new distillery in which to work. 'I was offered a job at Aultmore, near Keith, and we jumped at the chance of getting back to our local area,' he says. 'I went from brewer to production manager in 1994, and after a while the distillery was "twinned" with Inchgower, at Buckie.'

However, the remorseless consolidation that was taking place within the Scotch whisky industry saw Guinness plc, now the owner of the old DCL, merge with Grand Metropolitan plc in 1997 to create Diageo plc, and a legal requirement of this merger was that the new company divest itself of some brands to satisfy monopoly legislation. Accordingly, Bermuda-based Bacardi Ltd acquired the Scotch whisky business of John Dewar & Sons and the Bombay Sapphire gin brand for £1.15 billion in 1998 and Aultmore, Aberfeldy, Royal Brackla and Craigellachie distilleries were transferred to Bacardi ownership.

Aultmore was yet another product of the 1890s distilling boom on Speyside, but the distillery as it appears today betrays few signs of its heritage, due mainly to a 1970s expansion and reconstruction programme, which saw capacity doubled by the installation of a second pair of stills.

Gordon says that, 'After the split which took Aultmore into Dewar's, the distillery had to have its own production manager, and that was me. I did that job until I'd served my forty years and then I retired. I've seen lots of changes in the Scotch whisky industry in that time. Most notably, I think in terms of automation of plant, particularly in mashing and distilling. We had gone from everything being manual to a press of a button doing everything. There is a fully automated lauter mashtun at Aultmore, and controls for the stills were upgraded in 2008. However, the operator still has to make decisions himself. At the spirit safe he would read a hydrometer and thermometer to determine the strength of the spirit, and decide when to "cut" the flow of spirit. As for opening and closing the valves to empty and fill the stills, the operator still controls that, even though the actual valves are automatic.'

However, Gordon adds that, 'You could take a guy off the street who was able to work a computer, show him what to do, and he could mash. But it wouldn't mean he understood the process. The mashtuns at Aultmore and Dewar's "sister" distillery of Craigellachie can be controlled by the manufacturer in Germany via a modem, though this would only happen if the manufacturer had to upgrade the software or if some new plant was installed.'

Treatment of 'by-products' and distillery waste has long been an important element of the whisky-making business, with measures being put in place as far back as the late 19th century to prevent pollution of the River Spey with its lucrative salmon fishing trade. Early experimentation of evaporating the pot ale – the residue after the initial distillation in the wash still – to produce a concentrated 'syrup' took place as early as 1906 in a plant in the Speyside distilling community of Rothes, producing a spray-dried, powdered form of evaporated pot ale which was sold as fertiliser.

Aultmore played a notable part in further development work on by-products, when a processing plant was installed at the distillery in 1952, where a substance more suitable for incorporation into animal feed was developed. This led to the creation of a full-scale plant at the now silent Imperial Distillery at Carron. The various processes were refined over the years, and Aultmore came to have a 'dark grains' plant, which mixed pot ale and draff – the cereal residue left behind after mashing – to create dark grains, a highly nutritious cattle feed.

Gordon notes that, 'At Aultmore the dark grains plant closed in 1985, when I went there, and re-opened in the early nineties. It worked for four years, then the plant at Glenlossie Distillery, at Birnie, near Elgin, started up to handle draff and pot ale from lots of the company's distilleries, and the Aultmore facility was shut down for good in the mid-nineties and dismantled a few years later. Now all the waste is tankered away.

'It was just another part of the whole business of distilling to be lost at Aultmore. Now barley comes in malted, it isn't malted on site, and at the other end of the process, the new spirit is all filled into tankers and taken away for filling at Dewar's Westthorn site in Glasgow. The warehouses at Aultmore were demolished in 1996.'

When it comes to relaxing with a dram, Gordon is as 'on message' as most of his colleagues, retired or otherwise, and he says that, 'Personally, I like a twelve-year-old Aultmore or a Dewar's twelve or eighteen-year-old, but every whisky has its unique quality. It doesn't matter what you put in whisky if you enjoy it. It used to be unthinkable to put anything in malt, but I like it with water, and I drink a blend with American Dry Ginger.'

Musing on his lengthy career, Gordon sums up by saying that, 'When I started in distilling, things were pretty antiquated. For example, you had to physically go in and clean the mashtun. You kept old clothes to do that, nothing was provided, and afterwards you would hang them up to dry. One day one of the guys who had been cleaning the mashtun thought he would have a shower after doing it, so he stripped off and got into the underback to use the hose there. Unfortunately for him, just at that moment the manager appeared with a group of visitors.

'Distilleries had a bit of fun about them. The work was done, and while there was horseplay, there were no accidents. Everyone was happy at their work. Now there is so much health-and-safety legislation that you need a permit for everything. I'm not saying we shouldn't be safety-conscious, but maybe it's all gone a bit too far.'

Gordon's talk of 'horseplay' is common among distillery workers of the pre-health-and-safety era, with one anonymous former staff member recalling a colleague who had a habit of taking too many drams during the night shift, and subsequently falling asleep, to the mild irritation of his co-workers. One night they got their revenge by tying his feet to the grating floor while he slumbered, before climbing to the level above and pouring a glass of water over his face. He immediately awoke and tried to leap to his feet, only to fall forwards as though pole-axed due to his feet being tied to the grating!

Gordon concludes by saying that, 'I really enjoyed my forty years in the distilling industry and missed it for a while when I retired, but like everything else you get accustomed to it. Obviously I have seen lots of changes in terms of automation. I don't know what changes you will see in the next forty years. Will you see distilleries with no operators at all and just a team of maintenance men going from distillery to distillery? It's gone from being a cottage industry to a factory industry now. Big business, factory-style manufacturing. But if I had to do it all again, I wouldn't change much really.'

CHAPTER 5
Rodney Burtt - Glen Albyn and Glen Mhor

UNLIKE MOST OF THE WHISKY FOLK featured in these pages, Rodney Burtt is not a Scot, and his association with the Scotch whisky industry was not a lengthy one. However, his memories of working at Mackinlays & Birnie Ltd's Inverness distilleries of Glen Mhor and Glen Albyn during 1969/70 are so vivid and detailed that they more than merit inclusion here.

Rodney was born into a Lincolnshire Quaker farming family, with roots going back some 450 years in the Kesteven area. As a young man he was employed for a time by the National Farmers Union before becoming involved in the wine trade, subsequently working in London, Germany and France. However, at the end of 1969 Rodney chose to swap the lowlands of Lincolnshire for the Northern Scottish Highlands and a job in the 'Highland capital' of Inverness. 'I was keen to expand my drinks industry knowledge in a practical way,' he says, 'having previously learnt about the wine trade from the vines up, picking grapes in the Rhine region, in Burgundy, Beaujolais and Bordeaux.

'A relative knew Willie Birnie, owner of Glen Mhor and Glen Albyn distilleries, which was how I came to be there. After a while I was told that I was unlikely to progress too far as a southern Englishman in the slightly 'clannish' north of Scotland, and so I moved on to East Anglia and joined Victoria Wines in the drinks retail trade.' Rodney ultimately found a long-term niche as a typesetter, working in Lavenham, Suffolk, and today lives in retirement not far from Ipswich.

Speaking of his days as a trainee in the whisky industry, he recalls that, 'The western approaches to Inverness off the old A9 road occupy the east banks of the Caledonian Canal, and this community is called Muirtown Basin. Glen Albyn was the first distillery to be built within close proximity to Inverness town centre. The strong advantage of building a distillery at this point was the easy access by ships, which berthed within ten yards of the grain hatches. Glen Mhor, however, was not built until 1892.'

Glen Albyn was said to have been constructed on the ruins of the Muirtown Brewery, which had catered for the thirst of the men who laboured to build the Caledonian Canal, and *The Inverness Courier* for

10th January 1840 reported the opening ceremony of the fledgling distillery. An entirely new Glen Albyn Distillery was constructed in the mid-1880s, and in 1892 the trade journal *Harper's Weekly* noted that annual output had more than trebled within the previous five years, stating that, 'The growth of the business is largely due to the active management of Mr John Birnie, the manager and distiller, who is well qualified for the responsible position he occupies'.

It is believed that Birnie became frustrated in his ambition to gain a shareholding in Glen Albyn, and as a result, in 1892, formed a partnership with Charles Mackinlay & Co, whisky and wine merchants, of Leith. They acquired a site just across the road from Glen Albyn, establishing Glen Mhor distillery, which commenced production in 1894. The new venture traded as Mackinlays & Birnie.

The partnership was converted to a private company in 1906, with the participation of a major trade customer, John Walker & Sons Ltd of Kilmarnock, which held 40% of the shares. Some years later, Mackinlays & Birnie Ltd, with the intention of doubling output, replaced the small Glen Mhor mashtun with a larger one and installed two additional washbacks, but had not got round to putting in a second pair of stills when the First World War broke out. All malt distilleries were closed, in the interest of conserving barley, from 1917 to 1919, when Glen Albyn became a US naval base for the manufacture of mines. Mackinlays & Birnie bought Glen Albyn in 1920, and by 1925 had added a third still at Glen Mhor, operating both distilleries in tandem.

Rodney notes that, 'At that time, and until the Second World War, supplies for both distilleries, including peat from Orkney and some barley, were delivered by sea to the doors of the maltings; and Mackinlays and Birnie dispatched some of their whisky from the distillery quay through the canal to Glasgow. The distilleries had to close in the Second World War, for the same reason as in the First World War. Glen Albyn was silent from 1941 to 1945 and Glen Mhor from 1943 to 1944.

'Glen Albyn was on the downstream side of the Canal Bridge and Glen Mhor on the upstream flank, and they were to be my daytime working quarters for the next six months when I started there in late 1969. Arriving at them was neither colourful nor inviting. The outbuildings were constructed of stark blotchy granite of pinks and greys, and there was a cluster of metal hoists and chimneys jutting out at random. The major characteristic was the pagoda-shaped protrusion of the kiln, from which white smoke emitted at various intervals.

'Glen Mhor and Glen Albyn faced one another across the busy A9 at Muirtown. They abutted on the Caledonian Canal, at the point where it falls in a series of five locks into the Muirtown Basin. Loch Ness, part of this waterway which links the west and east coasts, supplied the water for both distilleries by way of a seven-mile piped linkage. There were six houses for occupation by workers at Glen Albyn and seven for workers at Glen Mhor. Glen Albyn had the larger site: seven acres, compared with four acres at Glen Mhor.'

At the time when Rodney was employed there, Glen Mhor and Glen Albyn distilleries were jointly owned by Mackinlays & Birnie Ltd and the Distillers Company Ltd.

William Birnie was a chartered accountant by training, and had taken over the family distilling business in 1936. He therefore worked alongside novelist, nationalist and Glen Mhor and Glen Albyn excise officer Neil M Gunn for a short period before Gunn resigned his position with the excise service in order to concentrate on his burgeoning career as a writer.

Gunn was based at Glen Mhor and Glen Albyn from 1921 until 1937, writing such well-received novels as *Morning Tide* and *Highland River* during the relatively large amount of free time which his duties afforded him. Gunn also penned the seminal book *Whisky & Scotland* (1935), in which he writes of Glen Mhor that ' ... until a man has had the luck to chance upon a perfectly matured malt he does not really know what whisky is.'

As Rodney notes, 'Gunn advocated the banning of blended whiskies because he was of the school of thought that malt whisky was pure and blended whisky was not. Mr Birnie was also an ardent admirer of the malts, but his view departed from Gunn's because blended whisky called on nearly ninety-eight percent of his warehouse stock. This high ratio of output was needed to keep business up and running.'

Rodney describes William Birnie as, 'The grand old man of whisky,' and remembers that he would 'arrive during mid-morning in his Riley Elf, wearing a Panama hat, tweed jacket and pale-coloured trousers, and usually accompanied by his Golden Labrador.'

As a young, southern Englishman working in a distilling environment in the Highlands of Scotland, Rodney met many fascinating characters, but inevitably he was treated with a degree of initial suspicion. Dramming provided the ideal opportunity to show that he could be 'one of the boys.'

'Distillery routines and their product offered "perks" and these were issued in a typically spontaneous fashion,' he says. 'These were distributed on a daily basis and several times a day, before festive occasions or any other excuse one could muster – weddings, births and so on. At lunchtime and near the day's end the stillman of the rota would issue free drams of new whisky to all members. These measures of one-fifth of a gill contained the strongest portion of the spirit at 111 degrees proof [63.5%abv]. In order to become a fully-fledged member of this completely new type of environment I had to show that Sassenachs were particularly "hardy" and could consume new spirit without flinching.'

Rodney's period of training consisted of spending time in each "department" of the distilleries, starting with the maltings, where he worked for a month. He remembers that, 'My first contact with a department overseer was in the malthouse where Willie Simpson held the leading position at Glen Mhor. Here was a jockey if ever I saw one. He had the shifty eyes of a thoroughbred and a long, broad, flattened nose with rippling bones to deviously sniff out other people's affairs.

'During our tea breaks Willie would bustle into the bothy and clamour for his "Medicine Cupboard". Was he ill, in pain or depressed, I asked myself? I offered help to this seemingly anxious man. However, with relief I discovered that the "cupboard", situated in a corner, revealed a host of expectations. Small, unmarked bottles lined two shelves off which Willie seized one insignificant bottle, twisted off the crown top and drank a healthy draught. Willie was soon restored by the uplifting reactions of new-make whisky from a seemingly neurotic person to a steady being.'

Rodney recalls that, 'Malting was distinctly the most strenuous part of the whisky-making process and presented a world of extremes in temperature. I recall one morning standing alongside a pile of peat, which was fuel for the fire underneath the kiln. The temperature was a steady 27°F [-3°C]. This was opposed to the ultimate conditions of heat in the kiln itself where the mercury registered 92°F [33°C]. Remember, this was the Scottish Highlands during one of the coldest Februarys since 1947.'

In the Glen Mhor maltings, the initial process of 'steeping' the barley in water to create a 'piece' was carried out in the same manner as most other distilleries at the time. However, Glen Mhor and Glen Albyn were unusual in being equipped with Saladin maltings, and the piece was placed in the Saladin Boxes where the rest of the business of malting took place.

'The Saladin Boxes *[named after that same French engineer who invented those war veteran tanks]* were introduced to Glen Mhor in 1949 and to Glen Albyn in 1961,' says Rodney. 'The former distillery was one of the first to have a box installed on a trial-run basis. A pair of these was operating in each distillery by 1962 and they proved to be invaluable until 1980 when production costs reached exorbitant heights against the economic returns of updated mechanical maltings.

'Each Saladin Box consisted of parallel, concrete walls, 60-feet long, eight-feet apart and six-feet high. They were joined at each end by removable iron gates, and the metal plates covering the floor area were perforated. The twenty tons of barley remained in this box for ten days, during which time the corn adopted its essential change in the enzymes from starch to malt.

'What happened visually was this. After six days, small rootlets formed at the end of each grain, where roots would normally have appeared underneath field soil. The sprouting end which would otherwise have produced the stem is called the acrospire. This should never develop as it would absorb valuable food and energy stored within the husk that we want for malt conversion. Therefore it was imperative that selected strains of barley were of the best nitrogen content. In other words, the distiller wanted more root energy rather than plant enhancement.'

The Saladin boxes represented an improvement on the hard, manual labour of the traditional malting floor, and Rodney explains how they operated. 'Above the iron gates, at the end of the box, spanned a solid girder-type bar which supported four massive worm screws, vertically attached. The whole frame was electrically powered to travel on cogs along toothed rails which ran along the top of the sides of the boxes.

'Every eight hours, when a box was full of corn, the mechanism set off on its journey at the rate of one foot for every twenty seconds. As the worm screws twisted round they lifted the barley from the bottom reversing the top surfaces. This was the modern aerating method of turning. The barley was maintained at the correct temperature of 62°F [16°C] and moisture content of twenty-seven-and-a-half percent was sustained by the "turning" process, together with jets of water. These sprayed on to the barley from behind the worm screws as they moved along.'

The maltings were one production area where Neil Gunn and his successors in the Excise service were not in evidence. This was because their involvement only began once alcohol was created. As Rodney puts it, 'The malthouse was the sole department in any distillery that ran completely free from double padlocks, deer-stalkers, saccharometers and hydrometers. The absence of piping everywhere was evidence alone that the malthouse was the least regimented part of malt whisky manufacturing. But there was a lot of discipline needed to maintain timing and quality so that the remaining departments could rely on the best quality barley for mashing.

'Some men had worked at the malthouses of Glen Mhor and Glen Albyn for over thirty years, and a great deal of pride existed. That indicated to me that however humble or basic you may feel the malting process was, to those men it was a vital way of life. They produced a special Scottish luxury for people who appreciated the best things in life. Meeting these Highland individuals in their own settings left a lasting, clear impression on my mind that still remains forty years later.'

Recalling time spent shovelling barley prior to steeping, Rodney goes on: 'The work was both hot and dusty, and we were required to wear muslin-lined face-masks. My colleagues would periodically talk in Gaelic during our monotonous task and then translate the outline of their conversation for my benefit so I never felt left out. This illustrates the considerate nature and general courtesy of the Scottish Highlander, sterling qualities which existed at least up until 1970.'

During the first week of March 1970, Rodney moved on to the mash house as a trainee under the care of Glen Mhor brewer Sandy Campbell. His opposite number across the road at Glen Albyn was Ian McDonald. As Rodney says, 'If the Scots bear grudges this is an understatement, for the Massacre of Glencoe still incites as much feeling today as it did in 1692! The two brewers never met unless accidentally, and items of communication were conveyed by other people with the strict instructions, such as "Give this note to him, laddie" or "Tell him not to be so churlish!"

'Sandy was a well-built man of rolling muscle, tending to be excessively flaccid around his neck. He wore a cap which concealed a sparse headline of tundra, and he met you with a generous, open expression, albeit with a pouting lip. Although this feature meant he could grumble and exaggerate, I found these rare occurrences. Instead, I always found him to be considerate and patient, and he taught me a great deal about both the practical and administrative sides of a typical mash house.'

From the mash house Rodney moved to what he describes as 'The department where responsibilities reached a peak,' in other words, the stillhouse. 'The overseer here was the highest paid member of a distillery. He was the stillman or distiller himself, who produced what was recognised as a long-term project, because what he manufactured did not manifest itself until his product reached maturity at least three years later, and sometimes as long as fifty years on rare occasions.'

Rodney remembers that, 'The Glen Albyn stills stood side-by-side on top of a brick platform underneath which used to be the fires. These coke furnaces presented many problems during the first distillation as the heat was concentrated in one area of the bowl of the still. If the distiller did not utilise 'rummagers' or revolving chains, the inside surface would burn. The updated method was another source of relief to me – the introduction of steam-heating through metal coils of piping inside the bottom of each still. These heated the contents in a more widespread and reliable fashion, along the same lines as an electric kettle. Rummaging, dust and dirt were out; speed and efficiency were in.'

No two single malt whiskies are identical, even if, as in the case of Glen Mhor and Glen Albyn, the distilleries producing them share a source of malted barley, water and casks in which to mature the spirit itself. The principal variable in this case was the stills, and Rodney maintains that, 'The size did not matter, but the shape altered the final texture of the distillate. Glen Mhor's stills were dumpy and as a result produced the heavier, robust malt it was famous for. Glen Albyn's on the other hand, were slender, bulbous vessels which subsequently made a lighter-nosed malt. No Glen Albyn had been bottled as a single malt since the Second World War, or, indeed, during Mr Birnie's term of office.

'Both Glen Mhor and Glen Albyn distilleries produced an intriguing and contrasting pair of malts. The former was a classic, heavily perfumed whisky and the latter much lighter and less aromatic. Glen Albyn was bottled as single malt for the Italian market which appreciated the care-free nature of the whisky. But after the Second World War Glen Albyn was not seen for forty years, and now only small stocks are becoming available in this century. Glen Mhor, on the other hand, was bottled consistently as ten-year-old until 1973 when the DCL withdrew it from the market for three years. The Glen Mhor malt re-appeared in 1976 as an eight-year-old under a different label, with mauve livery as opposed to the peat-brown original.'

We tend to think that the legacy of over-production which led to the closure of more than 20 distilleries during the 1980s, and accounted for both Glen Albyn and Glen Mhor, was not recognised until around 1980, but Rodney reveals that this was certainly not the case so far as William Birnie, for one, was concerned.

'He compiled extensive tables on consumption and production of potable spirits worldwide,' says Rodney. 'His tables of these statistics were publicised annually in the *Daily Express*. During the 1960s, Mr Birnie indicated to the trade that there were serious signs of over-production, but his counterparts observed him as over-sensitive and pessimistic. He told me personally in May 1970 that no-one would listen to his predictions and that various distilleries in the Scottish Highlands would close.'

By the time that Glen Albyn and Glen Mhor met their ultimate fate they were wholly-owned by the DCL, which already controlled 43.5% of Mackinlays & Birnie Ltd, through its John Walker & Sons subsidiary, with Walker having merged with DCL in 1925, along with Buchanan-Dewar Ltd. The distilling licences for the Inverness distilleries were subsequently held by DCL's Scottish Malt Distillers Ltd (SMD) subsidiary.

Nineteen seventy-two had seen DCL make a successful bid to acquire all the issued ordinary share capital of Mackinlays & Birnie Ltd other than the proportion it already held through John Walker & Sons Ltd of Kilmarnock. Mackinlay McPherson Ltd (a subsidiary of Scottish &

Newcastle Breweries Ltd) owned 10.9%, while the balance was held by 11 members of the Birnie family and 14 members of the Mackinlay family.

The offer put a value of £765,000 on Mackinlays & Birnie, and Rodney maintains that, 'It was welcomed by the directors because, they stated, the company had experienced difficulty in recent years: "The number of outlets for Mackinlays & Birnie's fillings has decreased due to greater integration within the industry and it is felt that this trend would continue." DCL, on the other hand, was ready to use the firm's spare productive capacity.'

This situation was not to last, however, and Rodney recalls that, 'During the latter half of 1982 the stark realities occurred as prophesied twenty years previously by the late William Birnie, who died in 1973, aged eighty-three years. Over-production had reached acute proportions in 1981 and it was clear that there was no alternative for the future of the two Muirtown distilleries. The last distillation was on 8th March 1983, allowing nearly twelve weeks' notice for closure. The day of 31st May 1983 is deeply imprinted on our minds as the distilleries closed. Bitterness was evident and despondency was prevalent, but to show their affection for their workmates a former stillman [Duncan McDougal] wrote this verse as a reminder of many happy distilling hours.

> The Distilleries are closing – that is the sorry news,
> As Birnie had predicted – there's a glut of booze.
> The workers at Glen Albyn and also at Glen Mhor
> Really were dumbfounded – shocked right to the core.
>
> Summoned to the Stillhouse to hear the Managers say,
> 'It's the end of the road for us – we close at the end of May.'
> No doubt there were some murmurs and questions coming fast.
> There was substance in those rumours – they've come true at last.
>
> So ends an era of forty years, no less,
> When Glen Albyn was a suburb of the town of Inverness.
> If these grey walls could speak, what a story they could tell
> Of the many varied incidents that happened in 'The Stell'.
>
> The roaring of the boiler is a thing of the past,
> And the mash going in on Tuesday has got to be the last.
> No more you'll hear the Malties cry, with an excuse to make you weep,
> 'Can't give you a hand just now lads – We're taking down a steep.'
> Everything is silent – the machinery is still.

No more loads of barley, no grist for the mill.
The Distillers Co may smile 'cos stocks are abundant,
But that is little comfort to folk who are redundant.'

Rodney goes on: 'However, worse was yet to follow. Management in its infinite wisdom chose to operate the remaining distilleries for storage purposes only. The whisky was drawn from bond, not to be replenished, and the emptying warehouses were rendered obsolete.'

During 1986, DCL was the subject of a hostile and hugely controversial takeover by Guinness plc, and Rodney remembers that, 'When the bitter struggle was over between Guinness and DCL it was hoped that they would mothball the closed distilleries for some years to come. But the final blow arrived in October 1986, when the building developers moved in.' Today, Glen Mhor and Glen Albyn have disappeared without trace, demolished to make way for car parking and a retail park.

'There was a terrific air of grief and frustration at the demise of two valuable Inverness institutions,' recalls Rodney. 'The anguish was exacerbated by the fact that William Birnie had given repeated warnings from the 1950s onwards that whisky production should be stabilised carefully to prevent over-production.'

Musing on the many distillery closures of the 1980s, Rodney talks of 'General apathy and mismanagement,' claiming that, 'the blenders refused to believe that one person could forecast the future of the malt whisky industry.'

Despite it being four decades since he worked at Glen Albyn and Glen Mhor, he retains an obvious affection for the places and the people associated with them. 'It is always a tragedy when a conventional era reaches the end of its cycle,' he declares. 'The fact that people thereafter lose their identities within their own workplaces is an endemic, depressing situation. The vital community spirit, where individuals could express their concerns and pleasures amongst themselves in the warmth of those closeted bothies, has long since become extinct.'

CHAPTER 6
Douglas Murray – Whisky Technologist

WHEN WE THINK OF WHISKY-MAKING there is a tendency to romanticise the whole business of turning barley in a field into spirit in a bottle, but a business is exactly what it is, and one that has increasingly come to rely on technological and scientific advances to ensure its prosperity. This is particularly true of large-scale production, such as that undertaken by Diageo, which owns the world's bestselling blended Scotch in the shape of Johnnie Walker.

Johnnie Walker is globally the leading Scotch whisky in terms of both value and volume, selling almost 18 million cases per year, and Diageo's Scotch whisky brands saw net sales total close to £3 billion during the financial year 2011/12. With growth running at around the 50% mark during the past five years, the company has invested massively in many of its existing 27 malt distilleries and its Cameronbridge grain distillery, as well as spending £40 million on an entirely new, vast malt distillery at Roseisle on Speyside during 2008/09, bringing their malt distillery portfolio to 28.

In 2012 Diageo announced its intention to spend £1 billion upgrading more of its distilleries, augmenting warehousing and building at least one new distillery of approximately the same capacity as Roseisle (10 million litres per annum), while preparing plans for another.

This is whisky-making on its most industrial scale and with increased efficiency, productivity and consistency, coupled with environmental sensitivity being the ultimate goals of public companies like Diageo, it may be argued that the unsung heroes of the modern Scotch whisky industry are actually scientists and technical gurus. One of the most respected such figures is Douglas Murray, Process and Liquid Technology Manager for Diageo Scotland Ltd. Douglas was born among the 'powerhouse' grain distilleries that were at the heart of the whisky industry in Central Scotland, where the likes of the now lost Cambus and Carsebridge plants were situated in Clackmannanshire, and Douglas recalls that, 'I joined the DCL on 1st October 1972, as a laboratory assistant at Cambus distillery. I actually joined the Scottish Grain Distillers [SGD] subsidiary. I was eighteen years old at the time.'

Cambus dated from 1806 and was one of the earliest grain distilleries in Scotland, converting from malt to grain production 30 years after its establishment. Cambus has a place in DCL history as of the six grain distilleries involved in the formation of the company in 1877. However, this did not prevent its closure during 1993, a decade after nearby Carsebridge had fallen victim to company cutbacks, and five years after DCL's great Caledonian grain distillery in Edinburgh also closed.

'DCL was well respected,' says Douglas. 'My father was very pleased when I got a job with them. My mother's family had a long distilling history, with lots of her cousins working in the Scotch whisky industry. Her great-great-grandfather worked in Port Charlotte Distillery on Islay. The family was from Islay, and came over to the mainland to work at Port Dundas Distillery in Glasgow when that opened in the early 19th century, eventually moving to Glenochil Distillery at Menstrie. Glenochil belonged to DCL and though it closed in 1929, most of the site has been retained and it's actually where I am now based. So it was through distilling that my family came to be in the Clackmannanshire area, and several of my cousins worked at Cambus.'

As is so often the case, Douglas got his first job at Cambus Distillery due to a connection with someone already working there, though in this instance it was actually the distillery manager. 'When I was in my teens I was a good athlete,' he says, 'and one of the coaches at the local athletics club was the Cambus manager, Donald Beaton. He heard I was looking for a job and he took me on.

'I turned up at Cambus for my first day's work on the 1st October 1972, but it was a local holiday. Nobody had told me. I was sent home by the gate man! I went back on the Tuesday only to find my boss, Mr Thorburn, didn't know anything about me starting work. The manager hadn't told him, and he didn't even know that anyone else was needed in the lab, where I was to be based.'

Formality was the name of the game within DCL, as it still was within most organisations at the time, and Douglas notes that, 'They were always addressed as Mr Beaton and Mr Thorburn, and everyone wore a tie to work, even in the lab. I had to go to a stationery shop and buy a fountain pen, because Customs and Excise insisted every ledger entry was in fountain pen.

'You would get visits from the top people in the company, and when Dr Forbes, who ran SGD, came around it was a big day. He would come round the site and say hello to everyone and then disappear into the manager's office for the remainder of his visit.'

Dr Magnus Pike, who found television fame during the 1970s as an

eccentric, arm-waving populist of science, was head of the research department when Douglas was working at Cambus. 'Once a week he came over
from Glenochil and nosed the spirit,' notes Douglas, who insists that,
'Overall, DCL was a caring company. It had a staff association as well as a
union. If you were "staff" you had a separate toilet to the workers, and you
got a key for it! There was a strict work ethic, as in almost all companies at
that time. You started work at nine am and finished at five pm. There was
no such thing as flexitime. They were good employers, though, and people
would spend their entire lives with DCL.

'After twenty-five years of service you got a prize – you picked something appropriate from a catalogue,' notes Douglas, 'and if you worked for
forty or fifty years you got a sum of money for a present, and a presenta-
tion was then made in the canteen. DCL was a family, and it was obvious
who your father was! You got parental advice rather than friendly conversation. By contrast, today's Diageo is a happy-go-lucky family.'

DCL was absorbed firstly through its controversial takeover by
Guinness plc in 1986, after which United Distillers was created as the spir-
its arm of Guiness. Then, as a result of the merger in 1997 between
Guinness and Grand Metropolitan plc, Diageo was created.

Back in the days of DCL, the powerful combine incorporated the six
most significant Scotch whisky brands of its day, all previously independent companies, and Douglas notes that, 'Each of the 'big six' Scotch
whisky companies within DCL very much retained its own identity, and
quite a lot of autonomy. The company was like a series of silos. You had
Buchanan's (Black and White) at Stepps in Glasgow, White Horse at Port
Dundas in Glasgow, Sanderson's (Vat 69) at South Queensferry, near
Edinburgh, Haig at Markinch in Fife, Dewar's in Perth and Johnnie
Walker in Kilmarnock. All the cask ends associated with each of the six
were painted different colours and stencilled with their names.'

Despite the fact that Cambus was not remotely located like many rural,
malt distilleries, 'When I started work there the distillery was a real community,' recalls Douglas, 'because almost everything was done in-house.
You had your own carpenter, plumber, engineer, painters, even the people
who cleaned our overalls. They were all DCL employees. Nothing was out-
sourced. Most of the houses in Cambus were owned by DCL, and the company also had lots of farms. Some were arable, but the majority had cattle
on them, in order to eat the 'draff' produced during distillation.'

Recalling Donald Beaton, the Cambus manager's abiding love of
sports, Douglas remembers that, 'He was into the shot put and they used
to practice in front of the distillery. But one day the distillery blacksmith
came past and Donald asked him if he'd ever thrown a hammer. He said

no, he hadn't, but he'd give it a go. Well, he threw it eighteen feet past Donald's best mark. The lads like me, we never beat Donald – it just wasn't done. We knew better. Not only did the blacksmith beat Donald but when the hammer landed it broke the water main and the entire distillery had to be shut down. After that, Donald and the blacksmith had anvil-lifting competitions instead!'

In common with all large distilleries, there was a significant HM Customs & Excise presence on the Cambus site, and Douglas recalls that, 'There was a surveyor and four officers, plus eight or more "watchers" or "gaugers". There was an almost military hierarchy within the Customs and Excise. As a distiller, you couldn't do anything without a day's notification. They effectively dictated what you did – if you wanted to do an extra mash or whatever, it required their permission.'

There were also some notably quirky aspects of the DCL operation, and Douglas explains that, 'We had fishing rights on the rivers Devon and Forth, and we had two fishing boats at Cambus Distillery. We had four or five miles on the north bank of the Forth, and two fishing beats at the distillery. Workers were sometimes sent out to fish for salmon or sea trout from the bank, and whatever was caught was taken to the CO_2 plant and frozen there. The fish came out like cricket bats!'

'They would be sent up to big hotels where DCL board members were hosting events. Usually the board members ate the salmon, and the sea trout were often cut up and distributed among the Cambus workforce as a perk. 'Members of the DCL board would go fishing from time to time and a Telex would arrive at the distillery office informing us when this was about to happen. We would stop mashing or whatever and go out into the fields and dig up worms and grubs to be used as bait. We had our own gardeners and they would prepare biscuit tins filled with straw. The worms were duly put into the tins, which were labelled by field and by distillery – it wasn't only Cambus that undertook this duty.

'One of the directors' chauffeur-driven Rolls-Royces would arrive at the distillery to collect the Cambus worms. I remember after one fishing trip to Oykell Bridge up in Sutherland we received a hand-written letter outlining which worms had performed best and instructing the gardeners and local farmers not to interfere with the fields where the best worms were produced!' If all of this sounds decidedly Victorian and patriarchal to anyone used to modern corporate life, it should be remembered that these events were actually occurring during the 1970s and early 1980s!

In terms of Douglas's own career he says that, 'DCL liked you to get a chemistry qualification, and I got my HNC in chemistry at technical college. Then, in 1975, a chemist's job came up at Cambus and I got the position. I did an Open University degree in chemistry and my title changed to Quality Manager, after which I moved into environmental management during the mid to late-1980s. In 1992 I transferred to the malt distilling side of the business, initially with a role in scrutinising spirit character.

'The Process Support department was created and I joined that around 1996 as departmental head. A restructure in 2003 saw me join the Process Technology section at the old Carsebridge Distillery site, and a year later there was another reorganisation, which created the Technical Centre Europe. This looks after all of Diageo's European spirits interests, and not just Scotch whisky.'

It would be easy to imagine that DCL was a very conservative company in terms of technical and scientific developments, but Douglas declares that, 'They were actually at the forefront of the industry in terms of innovation. They rivalled companies like ICI in that respect. They were not backward, far from it. There would be forty to fifty people working for the old 'research station' on the same Glenochil Distillery site where Diageo's Brand Technical Centre is now based. DCL was always very secretive, and would never tell anybody outside what it was up to. With the creation later of the Scotch Whisky Research Institute [SWRI] lots of research became industry-wide.'

On the topic of innovation, Douglas says that, 'When I started work in the whisky industry a mashman mashed, and the brewer told him how. In turn, scientists told the brewer. Nowadays, the technical ability of our individual operators is far higher. The mashman now knows all about enzymes and so forth. I've been a big part of the process that has led to that.

'In the Scotch whisky industry we portray ourselves as being very traditional, but actually we're quite pioneering. My great-great grandfather was Archie McNiven, who worked at Port Charlotte Distillery on Islay, and if we took him into a modern distillery he would probably recognise the stills, but not much else.'

Fundamental changes in the world of whisky-making have included the replacement of individual distillery floor maltings, where quality was variable, with large-scale, relatively automated dedicated malting plants, which make for greater consistency and are also more economical. Apart from any other factors, as distilleries were expanded during the 1960s and '70s, there was simply no way that floor maltings could keep up with growing demand.

Additional consistency was introduced by the replacement of direct-firing of stills by internal steam coils or pans, while yeasts were developed to give more efficient and controlled fermentation, and the cultivation of specialised varieties of malting barley have resulted in higher yields, both in terms of the actual crops and the amount of spirit produced from them.

Evolution of barley varieties is ongoing, but really began in the mid-1960s with Golden Promise, which was hardy, fast maturing and had superior malting attributes to its predecessors. It also had a short stalk, which meant it could thrive in more exposed and windy parts of Britain, and notably Scotland, where its introduction allowed distillers to use far more 'home-grown' barley than had previously been the case.

Perhaps the most significant change in the world of Scotch whisky concerns what may be seen as the final stage of production, namely maturation, with a greater understanding of 'wood chemistry' leading to much more rigorous wood policies, and consequently a higher quality and more consistent product.

The word 'consistent' keeps appearing in this litany of distilling changes, and Douglas declares that, 'It's a good thing if we can be more uniform. People want the Johnnie Walker Black Label blend always to taste the same. It's much easier to achieve that if the component malt and grain whiskies are always identical. This week's Lagavulin, for example, will be the same as last week's, thanks to the science. The blender can then concentrate on things like line extensions.

'We have built up fundamental knowledge of what the quality is about. We now know why each distillery makes the character of spirit that it does. We can therefore make a whisky "in the style of Distillery X", if not obviously identical to that of "Distillery X". Because of scientific research we understand why things are as they are.

'We allow the operators to react faster through use of computers, but none of our distilleries is fully computerised. For example, the operator will choose which one of ten available mashing programmes he wants to use, based on analysis of the malt and so on. And the same applies to the "cut points" in distillation.'

Douglas adds that, 'We can also make more alcohol now. We used to get six per cent strength in the washbacks, now we can get ten per cent from the same kit. You can get good yields in terms of alcohol potential compared to in the past. We have used the technology wisely to emphasise the good things and have paid due regard to history. It's not about losing mystique, it's about consistency. The new technology does not affect the character of the spirit.

In terms of raw materials, Douglas says that, 'When I joined the company in 1972 we used American maize and Canadian malted barley for grain spirit. We now use UK-grown wheat and barley whenever we can get it. We have used technology to be more traditional, if you like. We want things done in Scotland wherever possible, so we have good relationships with the farmers here.'

In relation to wood policy, Douglas notes that, 'In the past, casks were used three or four times, then thrown away. We can now measure wood extract by machine, so we can pin down the variables of wood. We are now getting up to five fills per cask, then rejuvenate it by 'de-charring' and 're-charring' for a further five. We purchase less wood, in effect, because we are using what we have much better than we used to. We measure the potential every time we empty a cask and eventually rejuvenate it.

'Essentially, we are a big business making big blends, so consistency and continuity are crucial; but every now and again the distillery makes something different, or a cask throws up an unusual result. Our technical system tells us when something is outwith normal parameters, and these casks are put aside for use as part of our annual Special Releases programme, or for use in our Johnnie Walker Blue Label blend.'

Regarding present developments, he says that, 'At the moment we take samples of wash from each distillery and analyse them in the central laboratory. In the next generation you will get that analysis taking place actually in each washback. We also have lots of ongoing environmental work, particularly in relation to dealing with pot ale, spent lees and draff. We are also now spending a lot of money and resources on researching the use of less energy and less water.

'You could work in the whisky industry for hundreds of years and still find there are questions unanswered because there are so many natural variables. The day I come to work and feel bored is the day I retire.'

CHAPTER 7
John Peterson – Production Director

TOURISTS HEARING OF LOCH LOMOND Distillery probably fondly imagine a bijou whisky-making facility, with maltings and pagodas and a pair of small stills, turning out a boutique, long-aged single malt of great rarity, lovingly hand-crafted on the shores of Scotland's largest – and most accessible – loch. The reality is, however, altogether more industrial in appearance and scale, despite the southern shores of the loch in question being only a short distance away.

Just before you turn into the road leading to the Lomond Industrial Estate where Loch Lomond Distillery is located, you pass a magnificent, red sandstone edifice, built in 1907 as the public face of the large factory where the long-lost Argyll Motor Co Ltd manufactured cars. Today, however, there is nothing behind most of the frontage – the site has been cleared, apart from some buildings that house factory shop outlets – and viewed from the rear, the old Argyll factory frontage resembles something you might find on a movie set. It is all image, and no substance.

Loch Lomond Distillery was built in the mid-1960s, as Scotch whisky sales soared, and the plant itself could hardly present more of a contrast. Pretty it is not. Functional and effective it most certainly is. Visitors are not encouraged – this is a place of work, not a whisky theme park. All substance and very little image.

The romantic Highland distillery myth-busting continues when you meet Production Director John Peterson. He wears a white lab coat – no tweed jackets here – and this is a clear sign of intent. John is a chemist by training and qualification, and at work he dresses like one.

Born in Edinburgh to a Scottish mother and a father whose family originates in Sweden, hence the Scandinavian surname, John studied chemistry at Edinburgh University. 'It was 1968,' he recalls, 'and it was the time when everyone was into rock bands. I didn't play in one myself but I spent a lot of time with people who did. After graduating I did teacher training, and then decided I didn't want to teach, so I went down to live with the band I'd been involved with at university, who were staying in a big farmhouse near Ipswich. I got a job in a factory making propellers, but that only lasted two weeks before I went to work as a chemist for Pauls Malt Ltd.

The band failed and the members all went back to Edinburgh. One became a librarian.

'I stayed in Suffolk with Paul's for six years before leaving to work as a research chemist in the new "jumbo" Whitbread brewery in Luton, which opened in 1976. But it was a terrible time for industrial relations and I left in 1980. The brewery closed in 1984 and the site is now a supermarket.'

Among the many brands owned by Whitbread & Co Ltd was Long John blended whisky, and John says that, 'This was served by the Strathclyde grain distillery in Glasgow and Tormore malt distillery up on Speyside. The chief chemist's job at Long John came up, but unfortunately for an Edinburgh man like me, it was based in Glasgow!

'I was there for about nine years, but I was lab-based and I wanted the chance to move on, but I felt I wouldn't be in a position to tell distillery managers what to do without some distillery experience under my belt. Therefore, when a job was advertised at Loch Lomond Distillery as Production Director in 1990, I applied and I got it. My intention was to do it for a year or two and then move on, but here I am still, twenty-two years later!'

The distillery had been constructed on the site of an 18th-century calico-dyeing factory, and John notes that, 'The old boiler house from the works was converted into the original production building of the distillery.' Loch Lomond made its first spirit during March 1966, and was equipped with a distinctive pair of stills, with long necks and internal rectifying plates, such as might be found in a Coffey still, instead of traditional lyne arms. These horizontal plates allowed for a variety of stylistic permutations, and were based on the 'Lomond still' design, developed in the mid-1950s by Hiram Walker & Sons (Scotland) Ltd and first installed in the Inverleven malt distillery, located within the company's Dumbarton grain distilling complex.

'There were several "Lomond-type" stills being built in the 1960s,' says John. 'I've always assumed it was because at that time industry in general was beginning to automate. Harold Wilson's "white heat of technology" and all that. Loch Lomond was built as a copy of Littlemill Distillery, which had the same type of stills and was under the same ownership. When I started at Loch Lomond in 1990 a couple of the malt operators had worked on site since 1966, and they said that the idea for the stills had come from the first manager, Duncan Thomas.'

Loch Lomond quietly went about its business of producing blending malt from the expansionist times of the 1960s until the "whisky loch" began to fill at an alarming level in the early eighties, and the plant fell silent in 1984. It was then acquired the following year by the Bulloch family – headed by Alexander (Sandy) – who saw it as a source of malt spirit for their blending and bottling operations, going on to re-commence distillation under the auspices of the Glen Catrine Bonded Warehouse Company in 1987.

The Bullochs can trace their involvement in the Scotch whisky business back to 1842 when Gabriel Bulloch partnered JH Dewar in a Scotch wholesaling business in Glasgow, and in more recent years A Bulloch & Co operated a substantial chain of retail outlets across Scotland, ultimately selling its own-label whisky, gin and vodkas.

This, in turn, led to the creation of Glen Catrine Bonded Warehouse Company Ltd in 1974, initially to supply bottled spirits for the company's 25 shops, but since their disposal, it has gone from strength to strength, and now produces in excess of 36.5 million bottles of whisky, vodka, gin, rum and brandy per annum, and Glen Catrine is the biggest independent bottler in Scotland. The firm is responsible for the fifth-best-selling blended whisky in the UK in the shape of High Commissioner, and the UK's second-best-selling vodka, namely Glen's.

The Loch Lomond side of the business – with an average stockholding in excess of 50 million litres of Scotch whisky – is the second-largest independently owned distilling concern in Scotland after William Grant & Sons Ltd, another family firm that likes to keep its business affairs to itself whenever it can. Indeed, when family-owned distilleries and whisky companies are mentioned, everybody thinks of William Grant, the Grants of Glenfarclas and Hedley Wright of Springbank. But quietly, and without fanfare or fuss, the whisky empire of Sandy Bulloch and his family operates on a notably large scale, albeit usually well below the media radar.

As John says, 'Essentially, it's an independent operation that does its own thing. If Sandy Bulloch wants to do something, he just does it. It's a family business, so not answerable to anyone else, and it can be very flexible. Sandy's wife Elsie is a Ballantine, so there's a real whisky pedigree there. Sandy is 86 now, but you still get told pretty quickly if you're doing anything wrong!'

In addition to owning Loch Lomond, Sandy Bulloch bought Littlemill Distillery at Bowling, not far from Auchentoshan, in 1994, when the plant was already silent, and it was decommissioned three years later, suffering a serious fire during 2004, after which it was demolished. Over in the old Scottish distilling "capital" of Campbeltown in Argyll, Bulloch added Glen Scotia Distillery to the portfolio in the same year as he acquired Littlemill.

'Both were bought principally to obtain their stocks of single malt, but we have been running Glen Scotia again since 1999,' notes John. 'Initially we majored in how we could get better flavours by analysing production methods and the new spirit, and by using good quality casks for maturation. A lot of investment is being made in the distillery now.'

Having acquired Loch Lomond Distillery principally in order to provide him with supplies of malt spirit for blending, Sandy Bulloch then decided in 1993 that he would also like an independent source of grain spirit. 'We used to buy five million litres of grain spirit from Strathclyde Distillery each year for blending', explains John, 'and one day they decided that they would only supply us with a much smaller quantity and at a significantly higher price. Sandy Bulloch said to me "You know about grain whisky, so build me a grain distillery!"

'The plan was that we needed five million litres of grain spirit per year, and I set out to make a grain that was fresh and clean, with no sulphur. A traditional "Coffey" grain still makes a heavier spirit, so we built stills that would make something lighter.

'The industry produces around 200 million litres of grain spirit per year. To me, grain is more important than malt in a blend. After all, there's a lot more of it in there. The principal and most important difference between grain and malt whisky isn't really about distillation methods, it's about flavour.

'Until the 1980s it was mainly maize, rather than wheat that was used to make grain whisky in Scotland, but maize became very expensive. The grain is pressure-cooked, which breaks down the proteins that contain sulphur as well as the other elements. We cook at eighty-five degrees centigrade – a lower temperature than most people, and we do it more gently. It still strips out the carbohydrates we need, but not the proteins, and it leaves the glutens unchanged. The result is "light and fruity" grain spirit. By contrast, North British grain, distilled in Edinburgh, would be considered "heavy". Coffey stills and high-temperature cooking give heavy and slow-maturing spirit, while the more modern continuous stills like ours make lighter grain spirit.'

So it is that today Loch Lomond has the distinction of being the only distillery in the country producing both malt and grain spirit under the stillhouse roof, but within the regime headed by John it has certainly not been a case of creating a grain distilling complex while allowing the existing malt distillery to carry on as before. Indeed, in excess of £15 million has been spent on the site while in Bulloch ownership, much of it in relation to the production of malt whisky.

According to John, 'When I came here we made 200,000 litres of malt spirit per year, now we make four million litres. In 1992 we installed a second pair of stills that were an exact copy of the first pair, which date from

1966. We used to have eight washbacks and now we have eighteen, plus we installed a new, much larger and totally automated mashtun five years ago. We have 300,000 casks on site in 28 warehouses and we run our own cooperage. All the processes are automated, and are operated by one man per shift, sitting at a computer screen.'

John defines the principal raison d'être behind the Loch Lomond operation when he declares that, 'We are here to make three-year-old blends. The company has always been short of spirit, and we need nice, light, fast-maturing malts for blending, and particularly for High Commissioner.' The main spirit type produced in the 'original' stills is named Inchmurrin, and is described by John as, 'Light, pure spirit, which is fruity and very fast-maturing.' He adds that, 'A heavier spirit called Glen Douglas is also made in the same pair of stills, using different cut points. This gives much heavier malt, which goes into Blue Label.'

'Blue Label' is the principal expression of Loch Lomond single malt on the market, though there is also a 21-year-old 'Black Label' and the intriguing 'red label' Single Highland Blended Whisky, which contains single grain whisky and a combination of some – or even all – of the eight different styles of malt whisky produced on the premises. 'Our blends are made with just one grain, our own, and virtually all the malt we use is our own, too,' confirms John. 'Reciprocal trading brings in just a very small percentage of "outside" malts.'

Heavily-peated spirit, deliberately distilled to retain heavier oils, is also produced in the 'original' Loch Lomond stills, with four weeks per year being devoted to distilling from malt peated to 50ppm and a further two weeks given over to making spirit from 25ppm malt. This peated spirit is named Croftengea, and it only rarely sees the light of day as part of the single cask 'Distillery Select' series. 'Croftengea is our most contaminated spirit,' John reckons, underlining his chemist's perception of whisky-making and clearly identifying him as not a native of Islay!

As well as adding a second, replica pair of stills, John was also responsible for introducing a third pair, which are as different in style to the originals as it is possible to get. 'We put them in during 1998 and they were my attempt to make a heavier and more traditional malt whisky. They are traditional-style pot stills, and we make a very heavy spirit in them, using Anchor dried yeast, which gives a weighty, estery spirit.

'We also make heavily peated spirit in them at times. This is all for blending purposes, except for very small amounts which are released occasionally in our Distillery Select series, when we call it Inchfad. It matures well in three years, despite being heavier than most of our spirit.'

Not content with these additions to the Loch Lomond distilling dynamic, John installed another still in 2008, and this was to prove somewhat controversial, to say the least. 'It is a continuous still which consists of two copper columns, encased in stainless steel. It was installed to make malt spirit and it can turn out more than the six pot stills together – around two million litres a year. We installed it simply because we needed to double output and there was no room for another six pot stills! This was the solution.'

Addressing the contentious nature of the new still, the mild-mannered, golf and piano-playing Peterson adopts an air of bemusement, saying that, 'It was put in around the time when the Scotch Whisky Association revised its definitions relating to Scotch whisky, which declared that malt whisky must be made in pot stills. It was all about the use of "traditional practice" in relation to distilling methods. Most malt whisky is made in what are essentially large factories, so what is "traditional" about that? Around twenty per cent of the malt in our blends comes from the continuous still, and if we want to bottle it as it stands we have to label it "Scotch grain whisky made from one hundred per cent malted barley."

'It's made in Scotland, it tastes like malt whisky, it's matured in Scotland for a minimum of three years in oak casks. It patently is malt whisky. It also saves a great deal of energy and is a very "green" way of distilling. One SWA objection is that it enabled us to make malt whisky much more cheaply than our rivals, and was somehow underhand.

'When we consulted our lawyers an advocate said that we were obviously right, but that the whole issue hinged on the contents of the 1909 Royal Commission findings. He told us we wouldn't win, so we didn't pursue it. The SWA said that how the whisky tasted was irrelevant. Presumably then you can make terrible whisky, provided it is "traditional". The SWA are Luddites.'

Unsurprisingly, Loch Lomond Distillery Company Ltd is not a member of the Scotch Whisky Association!

Above: Talisker Distillery as Norman Morrison would once have remembered it in the 1960s.
Below: A pensive Norman Morrison.

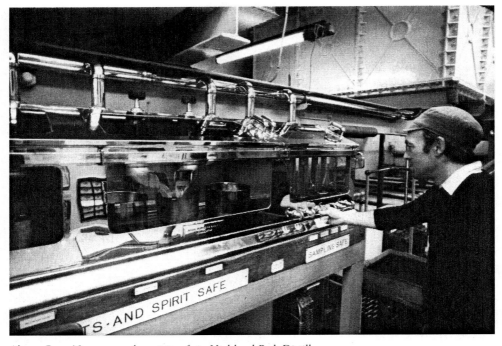

Above: Boyo Norquoy at the spirit safe in Highland Park Distillery.
Below: Jim Cryle with his infamous sma' still at Glenlivet Distillery.

Above: Gordon Dey, Aultmore Distillery.
Below: Gordon, back row, third from left, with the distillery staff in 1987.

Above: William Birnie (right) talking to Sir Ben Barnett, chairman of Mackinlays & Birnie Ltd, in September 1956.
Below: The laborious job of 'tapping' the casks for 'leakers'. The tone reveals leaking casks. Note the 1949 vintage of Glen Albyn in the hogsheads.

Above: Glen Mhor and Glen Albyn distilleries immediately on the right of the Caledonian Canal as it enters Muirtown Basin in Inverness. Below left: Rodney Burtt.
Below right: The Saladin Boxes were 60-feet long, eight-feet wide and held 22 tons of barley, couched up to three feet deep.

Above: The worm-screw mechanism travels along the length of the Saladin Box lifting the barley from bottom to top. Below: Russell McGregor, later the works manager at Glen Mhor, turning the piece in the 1950s. Saladin Boxes ended this practice.

Above: A mash commences with hot water entering from the sluice pipe at top left and the strirrers travelling through the mash. Below: A sample of wash is extracted in a dipping tin to be measured in a saccharometer for the level of gravity.

Above left: Douglas Murray. Above right: John Peterson at Loch Lomond Distillery.
Below: Stills bound for Benrinnes Distillery leave Abercrombie's in Alloa, c1955.

Loch Lomond Distillery: Possibly the most intriguing stillhouse in Scotland ... but there's something here of which the Scotch Whisky Association does not approve.

Above: Douglas Yeats (in apron) stowing barrels with fellow coopers at Dewar's, Perth, c1974.
Below: Douglas (7th from left at the rear) with Dewar's staff, c1978.

Above: Ginger Willie, Bowmore warehouseman, showing off one of his tattoos.
Below: His workplace. One of the dunnage warehouses at the distillery.

Above: Bowmore Distillery in the gloaming.
Below: John Ramsay in the Sample Room at the Edrington Group's HQ in Drumchapel.

Above: Glenrothes Distillery.
Below: Glenfarclas Distillery staff, c1891.

Above: John Grant in the Ship's Room at Glenfarclas Distillery.
Below: The stillhouse at Glenfarclas.

Above: Fred Laing shows off the Laing Brothers successful Big Peat range of blended 46%abv Islay malt whiskies. Port Ellen was Fred's father's favourite malt whisky and Big Peat contains malts down to 5-6 years of age.

Right: Fred with his father in 1952.

Above: Stewart and Fred Laing in their Glasgow office.
Below: The inspiration for the family business: Port Ellen Distillery, Islay, prior to its partial demolition.

PART TWO
Into the Wood

CHAPTER 8
Douglas Yeats – Cooper, Perth

PERTH IS A SETTLEMENT WITH ancient origins and royal heritage, centrally located between the Lowlands and the Highlands of Scotland. 'The Fair City' of Perth was therefore perfectly placed during the 19th century to capitalise on the burgeoning popularity of blended Scotch whisky, particularly as the spread of the Victorian rail network furnished it with very good transport links. Perth stood between the many distilleries of the Highlands and the markets of the Lowlands, England and beyond, and it soon became a notable locus for blending and bottling.

Perth was really put on the whisky map by three principal, rival companies, namely Arthur Bell & Sons, John Dewar & Sons and Matthew Gloag & Son of 'The Famous Grouse' fame. Of the three only Gloag, now incorporated into The Edrington Group, retains a presence in the city, having moved to purpose-built offices at West Kinfauns on the outskirts of Perth in 1996. Now part of Bermuda-based Bacardi Limited, John Dewar & Sons remains active in the county of Perthshire through its Aberfeldy Distillery and associated 'Dewar's World of Whisky' visitor centre.

The story of Dewar's is a fascinating one, with John Dewar, born near Aberfeldy, walking the 30 miles to Perth in 1828, aged 23, to work in a relative's wine merchants, before going on to open his own wine and spirits business in 1846, beginning to blend whiskies during the 1860s.

In the hands of John Dewar's two sons, John and Tommy Dewar, the firm thrived, with Dewar's ultimately becoming the bestselling blended Scotch whisky in the USA, a status it retains to this day. Tommy Dewar is renowned as one of the most colourful characters in the history of Scotch whisky, noted for his 'Dewarisms' such as, 'A teetotaller is one who suffers from thirst instead of enjoying it.' In 1892 he set off on a two-year sales tour of the world. By the time he returned he had spent the vast sum of £14,000 (almost £1.25m in today's money) but had established relations with 33 agents in 26 countries, and opened a branch of the firm in New York.

Flamboyant and with a great knack for self-publicity, which did sales of the company whiskies no harm at all, Tommy Dewar was effortlessly at home in the highest of society and was known for the phrase, 'If you do not advertise, you fossilize.' With this in mind, he was responsible for the first-ever motion picture advert for a drink, filmed by Edison in 1898. The film of dancing, kilted and quite possibly intoxicated Scotsmen was projected onto a building in New York's Herald Square and literally managed to stop the traffic!

From 1925 until its acquisition by Bacardi in 1998, John Dewar & Sons Ltd was part of the DCL and its successors, United Distillers and Diageo.

So much for the corporate story, but what about Dewar's on a more personal level? Husband and wife couple Douglas and Jeanette Yeats were both born in Perth at a time when several members of many families still worked for either Dewar's or Bell's. Douglas' sister, Helen, was employed in Dewar's bottling hall which was part of the company's Glasgow Road/Glover Street complex, where Dewar's landmark East Bond Warehouse had stood beside the railway tracks since 1912. Douglas says that, 'Jeanette, like many local girls, also went to work in the bottling hall after leaving school. Eventually, she was transferred into the bottling hall offices and became an export clerkess.'

Douglas was the son of a post office worker who had previously served in the Black Watch, the local regiment, which had its headquarters in Perth's Balhousie Castle, now the regimental museum. The Black Watch was a 'family' regiment, just as Dewar's and Bell's were 'family' blenders, with both achieving loyal support from several generations of local families.

'Growing up, there was a real sense that Perth was a whisky town,' says Douglas. 'Perth was at the hub of the wheel, if you like; a great geographical centre. The bulk of whisky came in by road from the Highland distilleries during my time. Dewar's was very family-orientated – you would get whole families employed by them. You would find mother and father worked there and perhaps a son and a sister, and you would get brothers together in the cooperage.

'When I left school I got a job as an apprentice cooper, based in Glover Street. The place was dirty and old, with wooden floors. I started at sixteen in 1958 and did labouring to harden me up, as it were, for what was to come. Today, they are all what I call "mechanical coopers", because so many of the processes are automated. When I started, your hammer and your "driver' were your main tools. It was heavy manual labour.

'It was a five-year apprenticeship, during which you were attached to a "journeyman", and you were his apprentice. Essentially, what you were doing was repairing barrels. Casks came in empty, they were checked for defects and you cannibalised others for staves to repair them where necessary. Rebuilding casks only came later when they started importing

Bourbon casks from the USA. By law they had to come into the country broken down into "shooks" *[component parts]*.'

Douglas remembers that, 'On my first day as an apprentice, my journey-man said to me that the initial thing you did when a cask came in was to put it up on end – there was always a chance there would be a wee dram still in it for me. One day we found four gallons of sherry in a butt that had come in from Cadiz in Spain. First-fill sherry casks like that were high-ly prized by the company.'

He explains that, 'Coopering was a very well-paid job. You were on piece work, for one thing. You were much better paid than the guys who worked in the distilleries. You could just about double your standard forty-hour week. But it was hard toil in the cooperage – you were well paid but you certainly worked for your money! There were incentives – you would get paid a bonus if you worked fast and handled more casks.'

Even today, when an apprentice becomes a fully-fledged cooper there is an informal ceremony during which he is usually rolled around the cooper-age in a barrel, having first been covered in a variety of unpleasant sub-stances. In the past, such ceremonies could result in newly-qualified coop-ers sporting black eyes and even gashes to their faces, but Douglas says that in the case of Dewar's, 'We would cover him in chalk and sawdust and roll him round the cooperage in a barrel, but it was never anything too haz-ardous. Though in some places there could be rough initiations.'

The period from 1959 onwards saw the development of a new bottling hall and blending centre for John Dewar & Sons Ltd at Inveralmond, to the west of the city of Perth, with a gradual transfer of equipment and employees being completed during 1962.

When it opened, Inveralmond was the most modern and productive facility of its kind in Scotland, and while seven bottling lines at Glasgow Road produced up to 1.2 million cases per year, at Inveralmond there were ultimately 22 bottling lines, capable of turning out almost four times as much whisky.

'The cooperage transferred to Inveralmond around 1962,' recalls Douglas, 'though they kept the big East Bond warehouse for storage after Inveralmond opened, and I had to go down from time to time to check for "leakers" and for slack hoops which needed tightening. That was the time when ex-Bourbon casks were first coming in. You had to re-assemble them and put new ends in. You had to make them a new, bigger size. We were taking them up to fifty-four gallons – hogsheads. They came in as a bun-dle of staves at American barrel size *[around 44 gallons]*. You raised them up; you brought them back to life again.

'Previously, they had used mainly ex-sherry casks and some port pipes.

The sherry casks we got came in as first-fills, not having previously contained Scotch whisky. They went off to Highland Park or wherever – they went to the malt distilleries to be filled.'

Douglas explains that, 'At Inveralmond I became a "journeyman" – I did two years 'on the bench' as they called it. I was sent over to work in the bond side of the operation when I was twenty-three because I didn't drink, and there had been problems with some of the guys working in the bond drinking far too much! It was just too tempting. Finally, I ended up as foreman cooper. As a "bond cooper" my job was to check casks to make sure there were no leaks, no damage at all. There was a blending floor in the bond. Casks came in from various distilleries by lorry and by train. They had their own train, with wagons being shunted in off the main line into a siding on the site.

'They brought in casks of Highland Park, Glenfarclas and lots of grain whisky, which came from all over Scotland. The first time I saw Highland Park it was a rich mahogany colour. They always wanted first-fill sherry casks for use in the Dewar's blend. The front office sent through orders for empty barrels for Highland Park, Linkwood and so on, to be used in five to ten years' time.'

The bond at Inveralmond contained between 2,000 and 3,000 casks of whisky that had been blended and then re-casked. 'The individual casks of whisky were disgorged into vats in the warehouse, it was aerated to thoroughly mix it and reduced in strength to seventy degrees proof,' says Douglas. 'It was then either re-casked or pumped directly to the bottling hall vats, depending on circumstances. Deluxe blended whiskies, like Ancestor, which was a blend of older whiskies, would be left in cask to mature for a while longer.

'Once the casks had been disgorged their ends were painted to show that they had been used once, and they were sent out as refill casks, unless they needed repair, in which case they went into the cooperage before being painted. Various companies used different colours – and Dewar's painted their cask ends a reddish-maroon colour. I had to examine the casks and see whether they were up to maturing whisky for another four to five years.'

'Sometimes you would do a specific Islay blend. All the Islays would be brought together and blended ready to be used in blended whiskies. You would only use something like two or three per cent of the Islay mix in a blend.'

No longer a non-drinker these days, Douglas has a fondness for whisky with a hint of Islay character to it, and his personal preference is for Dewar's old Perth rival – Bell's. 'The current version of Bell's has quite a strong Islay element to it, compared to lots of blends now, and that's what I drink,' he explains. 'I like the distinctive flavour of it.'

Compared to the basic conditions that had prevailed in the old Glover Street cooperage, Inveralmond represented a great improvement. 'In the bond you had a dedicated sweeper, and you also had a stone floor,' says Douglas. 'But it was all still manual, however. These days, coopers have mechanical hoop-drivers to save lots of the hard work and other such things.'

The modern equivalent to cooperages like that at Inveralmond is Diageo's state-of-the-art site at Cambus in Central Scotland, where all of the company's coopering activities have been concentrated since its opening in 2011. There 250,000 casks are processed each year, and the sort of robot-style technology more usually seen in car-making plants removes much of the heavy manual labour from the day to day lives of the coopers. Cambus employs 40 coopers out of the 200 currently working in the UK. As recently as the late 1980s the number was closer to 2,500.

Back in the days when Douglas was growing up, wooden barrels were still used to store and transport a wide variety of goods, including beer, and Perth was home to many coopers. He notes that, 'Coopers transferred from Bell's to Dewar's and vice versa, and also to and from Wright's Brewery [which closed in 1961], which used oak casks in the days before metal kegs replaced them.'

Recalling the Inveralmond operation, Douglas says that, 'At one time there were fifteen hundred people employed on the site. There were more than fifty just in the cooperage, including labourers. In the bond casks were stacked on top of each other and you had a mechanical lift to move them up and down. You had two rows of casks – one on top of the other. You had puncheons of one hundred and eight to one hundred and ten gallons, which were easier to handle and store. They were used for Islay blends, for Dewar's Ancestor and for the surplus from various blends. In those days Dewar's was in competition with the Johnnie Walker and White Horse blends, despite also being part of the DCL.'

While Douglas spent his time working with casks, most Inveralmond employees worked with bottles. 'The bottling hall was semi-automated at Inveralmond,' he notes. 'There were men at the end of the lines stacking cartons full of bottles onto pallets. The lines were mainly staffed by women, but with male engineers attached to the lines. Women would sit behind a screen, checking for defects and contaminants. They took turns doing that, because you could only really concentrate properly on it for an hour or so at a time. A squint label was not acceptable.

'The bottles came down the line already filled, capped and labelled, and the women manually put the bottles once checked into cartons. A woman was in charge of each line, making sure there were plenty of caps and labels and so forth for the machines.'

While today's Scotch whisky industry employs a significant and increasing number of women in production roles, until not too long ago if you visited a distillery and saw a female employee, the chances were that she would be typing letters or making tea. The bottling halls of the central belt were another matter entirely, however, with female staff traditionally dominating bottling operations, and often enjoying a fearsome reputation.

Strong men who could hold their own in most situations quaked at the prospect of entering the women's domain, and Douglas remembers that, 'When I was at Glover Street there was a washhouse, where used bottles were put into machines and washed with jets of water. Doing it like that was a big leap in hygiene and automation from when the bottles had previously been washed by hand. If you had to go into the washhouse the girls teased the life out of you. They were definitely not very ladylike! There were some wee characters!'

Despite being a relatively modern facility, Inveralmond was not immune to the vagaries of the Scotch whisky industry, and as Douglas recalls, 'Casks were stored at the back of the cooperage side of the bond, and we had seventy-five thousand on site at one time. Around 1974 we were getting the sense that they had been over-producing whisky. Casks were coming in full and being disgorged and then just stored rather than going back into the system.'

'Finally, the cooperage at Inveralmond closed in 1988, though the bonded warehouses remained in use and latterly the bottling hall was doing White Horse and various other DCL blends instead of just Dewar's. They were just bringing in the whisky by tanker, so no casks were being used then. When that happened it became obvious that the bottling hall could be closed – the writing was on the wall, if you like.'

As foreseen by members of the workforce like Douglas, the Inveralmond complex closed entirely in 1994, despite producing 4.4 million cases of whisky the previous year. 'The loss of Inveralmond was a huge blow to Perth,' says Douglas. 'I worked for Dewar's for thirty years, and well over a thousand people went when it closed and whole families lost their jobs. Coopering is a specialised trade and some of the Dewar's coopers transferred to Markinch, to the DCL Haig bottling plant there.'

Douglas opted for a change of career, however, noting that, 'I went into Bell's Sports Centre in Perth as a leisure assistant and did football coaching. I'd been doing football refereeing while working at Dewar's. Jeanette had left Inveralmond to have our first child, just before the place closed.'

'When I retired Jeanette and I went on a Mediterranean cruise and I finally got to see where the casks I'd worked on for so many years actually came from. I then worked in environmental health for Perth and Kinross Council and now I do deliveries for a local pharmacy, as well as playing golf twice a week when I can.'

As for the bigger picture of Perth's whisky heritage, the closure of Inveralmond was followed four years later when United Distillers & Vintners, the forerunner of Diageo, closed its Cherrybank offices in Perth, with the loss of more than 100 jobs, which were transferred to Essex. Cherrybank had been the headquarters of Arthur Bell & Sons, which lost its independence in 1985, and the demise of Cherrybank severed a connection been Bell's and the 'Fair City' that had last for more than 150 years.

'Today Famous Grouse at West Kinfauns is the last bastion of the whisky industry in Perth,' laments Douglas. 'At one time you had Gloag's, Bell's and smaller companies like Currie's and Thomson, who did the Beneagles ceramic whisky containers, as well as Dewar's, and now they're all gone.'

As always, however, small connections, coincidences and ironies remain. Douglas and Jeanette live in a house owned by The Gannochy Trust; AK Bell, son of Arthur, purchased the Gannochy Estate during the 1920s and proceeded to build 'model cottages for the deserving poor' between 1925 and 1932. Bell's philanthropic activities were formalised into the Gannochy Trust in 1937.

'There are about a hundred aand twenty houses in all and lots are rented by former Bell's staff' says Douglas. 'And there's us, who used to work for their big rival Dewar's, so there's still a whisky link in one sense.'

CHAPTER 9
Ginger Willie – Warehouseman, Bowmore

JUST AS SPEYSIDE REPRESENTS THE 'heart' of mainland malt whisky production, with around half of the country's distilleries within its boundaries, so Islay is Scotland's 'whisky island'. Although Islay is just 240 square miles in size, and only has a population of around 3,000 people, it is home to eight operational distilleries. During recent years its single malts have attained a near cult status among the world's whisky drinkers.

Islay is the southernmost of the Inner Hebrides, and lies just 25 miles north of the Irish coast. Its 'capital' is Bowmore, which was established by the island's owner, Daniel Campbell of Shawfield and Islay, in 1768. It was one of the first 'planned' villages in Scotland, and sits on the eastern shore of Loch Indaal.

Bowmore Distillery was founded in 1779, possibly earlier, making it one of the oldest in Scotland, and the first licensed distillery on Islay. Over the years it has been owned by a number of companies, but today is in the hands of Morrison Bowmore Distillers Ltd, itself a subsidiary of the Japanese whisky giant Suntory, which has owned the business since 1994.

One of the dozen production-related employees at Bowmore is Willie MacNeill, universally known as 'Ginger Willie.' He explains that, 'I used to have red hair in my younger days, and when I joined Bowmore Distillery the assistant manager, who was a cousin of mine, had the same name. He said I would have to have a nickname, so I just said "call me Ginger Willie," and it stuck. I'm an Ileach born and bred and very proud of it. My grandfather and great-grandfather both worked at Ardbeg Distillery and my mother's family were all born there.'

Like so many Scottish islanders, Willie joined the Merchant Navy after leaving school. 'I spent two years in that before coming home and starting work at Ardbeg in 1969,' he says. 'I started as a labourer and became head warehouseman there. I was there till 1976 when Ed McAffer, who was Bowmore's brewer at the time, asked me if I would like to work at Bowmore. He headhunted me! I lived in Bowmore so it was handy. I spent two years in the malt barns and then in 1985 they asked me to look after the warehouses. It was just a temporary job until they could get somebody else, but I'm still doing it more than quarter of a century later!'

Ed McAffer is now distillery manager at Bowmore, which is one of only a handful of Scottish distilleries still operating its own floor maltings, with three currently in use. They provide up to 40% of the distillery's malt requirements, with the rest being sourced from the mainland.

Within the spectrum of Islay malts, Bowmore is 'middle-of-the-road' in terms of its peatiness, being peated to around 25ppm. At the upper end of the phenolic scale, Ardbeg routinely peats its malt to 55ppm.

The Bowmore maltings require peat to dry and flavour the malt, and Willie notes that, 'I've been cutting peats for fifty years. Originally we cut all peats for Bowmore by hand. You started in March and you finished in September. One other guy and I would spend seven months a year doing it. I did that before I became head warehouseman.'

Peat was also an important source of domestic fuel for the people of Islay, some of whom still harvest it, and Willie says that, 'All families would go out at the peat-cutting. The "lots" were a mile from the village, and that's where Bowmore cuts its peat still today.

'You cut it in May or June and it lies for a week, then you stack it as it dries to let the wind get through it. The top turf gives you the best aromas during malting. It gives good smoke, which is what you really want. Further down is more like coal because it is older. It has heather and trees in it. You get different aromas coming off it compared to the peat cut in the middle of the mainland because of the closeness of the sea to it.'

'When it's cut by machine the machine sucks it out from under the very top layer and puts it out in "sausages". When it's hand-cut it holds more moisture. The machine can cut two hundred tonnes in a short time. In the old days, you would bury the wooden-handled tools in the peat bog until next time to keep the wood from drying out.'

Having been involved in one of the very earliest stages of whisky production, namely cutting peat for malting, Ginger Willie's current role in charge of warehousing places him at the opposite end of the whisky-making process, – that is maturing the spirit. Bowmore currently fills around 20% of its output into ex-sherry casks, and the remainder into ex-Bourbon casks, and the entire 'make' is now destined for single-malt bottling rather than blending. Some of the fresh spirit is tankered to the mainland, but the majority is matured on site, where a total of around twenty-one thousand casks are stored, with the oldest dating from 1958.

'You don't get the same whisky when it's not matured on the island, declares Willie. 'There's a heavy sea air and no pollution. We have galvanised hoops on casks here because the old mild steel ones rusted, the salt air affected them. Those sorts of conditions are bound to have a little effect on the whisky.'

'Number One warehouse was the first warehouse to be built when the distillery was established. It is partly below sea level and you get very little temperature change in it. During the winter, when it got down to minus eight degrees outside, it was appreciably warmer in the number one warehouse. It mainly houses sherry butts. 'To me, the ideal warehouse has thick, old walls and is slightly below sea level. You get damp, salt air. Evaporation is slower than in the big, modern ones. You don't lose as much spirit through evaporation as you do in the middle of the mainland.'

Traditional stone or brick-built warehouses with cinder flooring and wooden stowing to allow casks to be stored three-high are known as 'dunnage' warehouses, while more recent structures tend to be 'racked,' facilitating a greater concentration of storage. Many modern warehouses are 'palletised,' making for much easier handling with fork-lift equipment.

In a dunnage warehouse there will be a greater loss of strength rather than volume during maturation due to the prevailing conditions, compared to a racked or palletised warehouse, and there are fewer maturation variables from cask to cask. However, Willie says that, 'At Bowmore, warehouse number six is racked rather than dunnage, but I don't think you get too much difference, although it's damper in the dunnage ones.'

On a practical level, Willie notes that, 'I supervise the fillings, and we tap the casks, repair leakers, and check hoops. It's about upkeep and security. We don't just forget about the casks once they are in there. And where casks come out of the warehouses, new whisky goes into that space a week later.

'There weren't any hoists or fork-lifts in the old days in the warehouses; it was all guys pushing casks up wooden runners. Even today, rolling a half-tonne butt is physically hard. But they get used to pushing and controlling them. They can roll them so that they always end in position with the bung up – it's just practice.

'At Bowmore during the last twenty years we've got into spending lots of money on wood. All wood now is ex-first fill. You get the benefit at the beginning. Now the fifteen and eighteen-year-olds are very good whiskies. Overall, Bowmore has a great range of whiskies, and there's a big market for the twelve-year-old in particular.

'Bowmore is a middle-of-the-road Islay, not too heavily peated. Just right in my opinion. It's not too peaty but it's still got the Islay character. Islays are entirely different from whiskies made anywhere else in the world. My personal favourite is the Bowmore fifteen-year-old, which is a lovely, sweet, mild dram with a lasting taste when drunk neat on a winter's evening.'

The growing fashion for single malts during the past two or three decades represents a great contrast with drinking habits when Willie was younger, and he says that, 'When I started at Bowmore, virtually all the whisky we made was for blending. There were hardly any single malts around twenty-five years ago. Bowmore went into J and B Rare, Johnnie Walker, Haig and Chivas Regal. Chivas was a big customer when I was first here.

'Even on the island it would all be Haig, Johnnie Walker and maybe Black Bottle that was being drunk. If there was a single malt it would have cost a fortune. Usually we would have a pint of beer and a Johnnie Walker Red Label.'

Willie reckons that Bowmore Distillery has not changed dramatically in terms of the way it operates, though today a dozen production workers are employed where once there were around 30. 'There are fewer guys in the maltings now for one thing,' he notes. 'Instead of the malt all being turned by hand there is a now a turning machine, which means one guy per shift can look after all three malting floors. But the place isn't controlled by computers like some distilleries, and all the "cut points" on the stills are done manually by the operators.

'One of the main changes is that we're making a lot more whisky than we used to. We're now making whisky for tomorrow. There have also been environmental changes. We used to burn eighteen to twenty tonnes of peat per week in the kiln with big, blazing fires. That's now down to two-and-a-half tonnes per week. We cover the blazing peat with "caff," it's damped down with dust, in effect, to keep it smouldering.'

Away from the distillery, Willie declares that, 'Islay hasn't really changed too much over the years and we want to keep it as it is. Young people get a good education here but then they have to go to the mainland to find work. My two daughters are in Glasgow. It takes twenty minutes in the air ambulance from Islay to hospital in Glasgow, but it can take more than that time for an ambulance to get from one side of Glasgow to the other.

'There are more holiday homes than there used to be, and in the last twenty years the number of "whisky tourists" coming to the island has been amazing. All the distilleries conduct tours and the hotels, bed and breakfasts, shops and other traders all get something out of it.'

The downside of this increased traffic to and from Islay is that the pair of car ferries operated by CalMac between the Kennacraig terminal in Argyll and the Islay terminals of Port Askaig and Port Ellen became over-booked, with distillers complaining that sometimes specialist tradesmen and equipment could not reach the island when required.

CalMac's response was to invest £24 million in the Gdansk-built MV *Finlaggan*, which came into service during the summer of 2011. 'It can carry up to five hundred and fifty passengers and eighty-five vehicles and they are using it along with the *Hebridean Isles*, which was one of the two smaller ferries that used to work the route.'

Along with the employment of fewer members of production staff at Bowmore and virtually all other Scottish distilleries, older and retired employees tend to mourn the passing of many of the 'characters' who used to be involved in the business of making whisky. Perhaps in our modern, 'globalised' world with its increased homogeneity there is less room for true individuals and a greater desire to 'fit in.'

'When I first started working, there were lots of characters,' says Willie. 'They would have their drams every day at work, go home on a Friday night, and hand their pay packets to their wives. The wives would give them some beer money out of it for Friday and Saturday evenings. They did that and they had their drams at the distillery and they lived into their eighties and nineties.

'The dramming was done so that people wouldn't help themselves, or that was the idea, anyway. When dramming stopped they were given a free bottle a month instead. But you'll notice that there are no security cameras around the distilleries. If you stole whisky, casks of it, I mean, where could you take it? In Glasgow you could steal it at night and it could be in France by the morning!'

One thing that does not change on Islay is the winter presence of geese, with tens of thousands of Greylags, Barnacles and White-Fronted geese migrating south from the Arctic. Such are the numbers of geese wintering on Islay now that Scottish Natural Heritage pays farmers compensation for allowing the geese to graze on their land. 'I see them flying in during September and October, notes Willie, 'and I say "winter is on its way". They attract lots of birdwatchers from England, and there are choughs and corncrakes on the island, too, and they're rare enough now.'

In terms of his continuing employment, Willie says that, 'If I didn't love the job I wouldn't still be doing it. But you also get security and regular money and a pension and holidays. When I started at Ardbeg I was getting six or seven pounds per hour, which was a lot of money then. If we earned now what we earned in the suxties in real terms we'd be millionaires!

'My wife and I always go on holiday to Eastbourne each year, and I get a new tattoo every time I go. I pay for them in whisky. I've got twelve now, including one on my forearm that says "Ginger Willie" in Japanese. Away from work I love trout fishing and I'm a season ticket holder at Rangers, and despite the distance I go once or twice a month. I can go on the ferry for one-pound return now that I'm over sixty!'

PART THREE
Blending It

CHAPTER 10
John Ramsay – Master Blender, Edrington Group

DESPITE THE GREAT AND APPARENTLY ever-growing interest in single malt Scotch whisky, it remains a fact that some 90% of all Scotch consumed around the world is drunk in blended format. The Macallans and The Glenlivets, the Glenfiddichs and the Ardbegs may garner a disproportionate number of media column inches, but blended Scotch whisky is still king.

In particular, many of the 'emerging' markets, and especially those in Asia, on which so much ongoing faith is being pinned for the future prosperity of the Scotch whisky industry are not particularly interested in single malts, and may never be to any serious extent.

It follows then, that the select band of men and women who can lay claim to the title of Master Blender are precious people indeed. One such Master Blender – now with the tag line 'Emeritus' – is John Ramsay, who filled the top blending role at The Edrington Group for the last eight years of his 40-year whisky-related career, until handing over the baton to his understudy Gordon Motion in 2009.

'I was born in Glasgow in 1949', says John, 'and when I was ten years old my parents moved to Easterhouse.' This was a large housing scheme, created from the 1950s onwards, half-a-dozen miles east of Glasgow to provide accommodation principally for families who lived in condemned tenements in the east end of the city, but it soon came to symbolise a range of social problems all its own.

Gang culture was rampant, and at one point the high-profile popular singer Frankie Vaughan became involved in trying to attract more facilities to Easterhouse and defuse tensions between rival gangs, brokering a weapons amnesty and donating funds from his concerts at the Glasgow Pavilion to local youth projects.

'If you had two kids, when one of them got to ten you got a bigger house, and we were one of the first families into Easterhouse,' explains John. 'It has since become notorious, but I wasn't really aware of the gangs when I was growing up, partly because I didn't go to school in Easterhouse itself. I was in my teens at the time of Frankie Vaughan's visit.

'I was reasonably academic, but by 1966 I had discovered birds and booze and I only had one Higher qualification, which was not as many as I should have got! I decided to leave school and I wanted a chemistry career, but not by going to university as originally planned. I went into part-time education and was offered a job at Strathclyde Distillery. The lab where I worked was a "bridge" between Kinclaith malt distillery and the main grain side of the place.'

Strathclyde, a grain distillery, had been built by Seager Evans & Co Ltd during the 1920s in the Gorbals district of the city, an area with a historically more notorious gang culture than Easterhouse! It was soon providing the bulk of the grain requirements for the Long John blend, and in 1957 a small malt distillery, Kinclaith, was installed, in order to provide another malt strand for blending, but Kinclaith closed in 1975 to make way for expansion of the grain distilling operation.

'Kinclaith made less than one million litres per year and it wasn't a spectacular whisky,' admits John. 'It was designed as a "packer" malt for blending. There were maltings on site at that time, too. I was a lab assistant and was given day-release to get Part 1 of my Royal Institute of Chemistry qualification.'

After his time at Strathclyde Distillery, John worked outside the whisky industry for three years, acting as a lab technician in the chemistry department of Coatbridge Technical College, before joining a local whisky bond as an industrial chemist.

'Hall and Bramley ran the bond and they were agents for new-make whisky in the north of England,' says John. 'It was still common for publicans to take their own fillings then and have their own blends. Hall & Bramley were based in Liverpool. They dealt with The Macallan, Glen Grant, Highland Park, Glenrothes and Tamdhu malts and North British grain.' Hall & Bramley also acted in association with the Italian vermouth firm of Martini & Rossi, whose Scotch whisky interests were operated by their William Lawson & Co Ltd subsidiary.

'Hall and Bramley moved the whisky production side of Martini and Rossi to Coatbridge in 1968,' notes John. 'They did the whisky blending for Martini and Rossi. The operation got bigger and bigger, and they eventually needed a laboratory, which was when I got the job.'

'It got me back into the whisky industry and Paul Rickards moved north from Liverpool to run it all. He said, around 1971, that he would teach me the blending side of the business. Paul then joined Robertson and Baxter Ltd, a couple of years later, as their Master Blender, and William Lawson decided to employ its own blender, Hamish Robertson, who had previously blended for William Grant and Sons. I was asked to change employer from Hall and Bramley to William Lawsons, but stay in the same place. Hamish left in 1981 and I took on the Master Blender's role full-time, doing the job for nine years, until 1990.'

When it came to perfecting the complex and demanding art of whisky blending, John says that, 'Learning to blend was "hands-on", or rather "nose-on". It involved nosing a range of whiskies, initially just grains, to determine the differences between them, how North British differed from Invergordon, for example. Then I progressed to the spectrum of character of single malts. From there you learnt maturation, how to nose the whiskies at different ages, learnt the "template" for what different ages brought to the spirit.

'We did grains first, because they are generally less complex, then malts – from refill hogsheads, or "hoggies" and butts, from American oak and European oak. Then we built up to how these various whiskies at different ages interact with one another. I had to learn about mixing peaty whiskies – how much you use in a blend, and things like that. It was about listening and learning as much as anything, and finally being allowed to put stuff together – being told you had used too much of one, not enough of another, and so on. I learnt by trial and error and by supervision.

'At William Lawson's there was the standard blend, then an eight and a twelve-year-old, the latter being sold as William Lawson's Scottish Gold. As a malt we had Macduff, distilled just outside Banff and sold as Glen Deveron. It was a five-year-old, designed to mimic Glen Grant in the lucrative Italian market, and there was a ten-year-old. You saw the influence of better quality casks in the ten-year-old. At that time, William Lawson still "married" their whiskies, and they did it at full strength. They mixed grains and malts and didn't dilute them prior to marriage.

'At Robertson and Baxter we diluted the blend to forty-six per cent and then married it. For me blending is about using malt, grain and water. I think diluting it like that gives a better blend, particularly in terms of texture. Chill-filtration affects texture, though it doesn't affect flavour so much.'

In terms of changing to the blending regime, John notes that, 'Over time, as an industry we came to use fewer component malts in our blends, and there has been a change in that people now clean plant more thoroughly, so there is more control and more uniformity of malts. Stills don't boil over as they sometimes did when heated by coal rather than steam, and overall there just aren't such big variations in spirit character from batch to batch as there used to be. Consistency is very important for blending.

'Robertson and Baxter weren't into too many component malts anyway. Cutty Sark and The Famous Grouse contain fewer different malts than some of their competitors. I always say that if you take all the colours of the rainbow, you end up with white light!

'You have core malts in any blend – in our case Highland Park, The Macallan, Glenrothes and so on – and you would use others such as fifty hoggies of six or seven-year-old Glen Spey, then replace that with fifty of Strathmill, perhaps, when they were used up. You would interchange malts like those two, with similar profiles. I instigated that practice and saw no reason to change it.

'People became much more knowledgeable about wood, but Robertson and Baxter had always been keen to use decent quality wood and had a rigorous cask-rejection policy. They were doing this even before wood chemistry was well understood. We had less understanding of why it was important, and it was work carried out by the Scotch Whisky Research Institute over the years that helped us all to comprehend it better. A big part of the blender's job now is to establish a wood policy for each brand. You always had to have a long-term strategic eye to filling for the future.'

In 1990 John joined what was then known as Highland Distilleries Ltd, where he was employed as Production Controller. 'I worked on the distilling side, and part of my role involved input into new -make spirit quality. I had the sensory background to do this.'

William A Robertson had set himself up as a whisky broker in Glasgow during 1855, going on to establish Robertson & Baxter Ltd five years later, with bonding and bottling activities ultimately being added to the firm's 'middleman' role.

Later in the century, the firm took the next logical step and became involved in actual whisky production, with William Robertson being one of the founding partners of the company that built Bunnahabhain Distillery on Islay in 1880-1. Robertson & Baxter also went on to have an involvement in the Speyside distillery of Glenrothes and were instrumental in the establishment of the Highland Distilleries Co Ltd in 1887, with William Robertson serving as one of its original directors.

Highland Distilleries proceeded to acquire Glenglassaugh Distillery at Portsoy, on the Moray Firth coast, and Tamdhu, in the heart of Speyside, while James Robertson became head of both Robertson & Baxter and Highland Distilleries in 1898, following the death of his father.

Nineteen thirty-six saw Robertson & Baxter supply the first blend of the revolutionary, pale-coloured and light-bodied Cutty Sark brand, which was specifically targeted at post-prohibition North America, while Highland Distilleries bought Highland Park Distillery in 1937. The latter firm became a blender in its own right in 1970, with the purchase of Perth-based Matthew Gloag & Sons, owners of The Famous Grouse brand.

Meanwhile, in 1961, the three Robertson sisters who had inherited the Scotch whisky business built up by their family, established The Edrington Group, named after a farm near their home, and formed the Robertson Trust.

As far as John was concerned, 'Paul Rickards retired at Robertson and Baxter and I was offered his job in 1991. From then on I was Master Blender for The Edrington Group.'

Edrington and Highland came together in 1999, when Highland Distillers Ltd, as it had become, was bought for £601 million by a partnership comprising the Edrington Group Ltd, who were the major shareholders (70%), and William Grant & Sons Ltd (30%). Highland had previously acquired the Glenturret and Macallan distilleries, while Robertson & Baxter owned Glengoyne Distillery in Stirlingshire, having bought Lang Brothers in the mid-1960s. John's role of Master Blender had come to embrace the use of some of the highest-profile malt whiskies in Scotland.

'The Famous Grouse only came to The Edrington Group in the early seventies,' he says, 'and I don't imagine it would be much different in character now to the old days before that, when Matthew Gloag and owned the brand. They would probably have been filling Macallan and Glenrothes anyway, along with North British grain whisky. I started working on Grouse in 1991 and there was no policy to change those fillings. Grouse today should be very similar in style to the way it was in 1970.'

As well as more consistent spirit, better wood polices and a progressive reduction in the number of component malts, one other significant alteration to the Master Blender's role is that he, or she, has been dragged out of the anonymous shadows of the blending lab and given a higher, public profile.

'Today, the blender has a public face and that's very important now, and he or she is also asked to produce far more products, far more range extensions and special bottlings.

'When I took over as Master Blender we had two or three variants of age with Cutty Sark, we had Grouse, and we had single malt bottlings of Glenrothes and Highland Park and a Tamdhu. Macallan came in later. It snowballed through the mid-nineties in terms of new products. One of the first was the aged version of The Famous Grouse, which became Gold Reserve. Then it was single malts.'

While the role of Master Blender is popularly seen as being confined to the creation and continued development of Scotch whisky blends, ask any of the current high-profile occupants of the position, such as Richard Paterson, Brian Kinsman or Rachel Barrie, and they will tell you that a very significant, and high-profile, part of their role is in relation to single malts, and particularly the creation of new expressions of those malts.

One of the developments with which John was particularly strongly associated was the creation of an ongoing range of vintage expressions of The Glenrothes. Rather than just bottle another 12-year-old, for example, it was decided to opt instead for the wine industry model of releasing vintages, working on the basis that maturity, rather than age, is what really matters. 'This involved a lot of hard work but it was very satisfying to do that. It also gave me great satisfaction to work with iconic malts like Highland Park and The Macallan.'

When it came to the increasing number of product innovations, John says that, 'It was usually eighty per cent a case of the marketing people coming to me and wanting new things for brands within the portfolio – to cover new price or age points – and twenty per cent of the time the ideas were mine.

'The sheer growth in The Macallan hadn't been foreseen. There had, after all, been an eighties' downturn in distilling and The Macallan had been no exception. So there was a big inventory gap from the early eighties, which meant we were using a lot of 1979 whisky. There was serious over-ageing as a result of the shortage. If the whisky wasn't there it wasn't there – though that didn't stop a marketing man asking me once if we couldn't make some more eighteen-year-old!

'Part of my job was to keep the costs down and the product balanced, too, so things like the use of over-aged whisky aren't ideal. We ended up buying back stocks of The Macallan from rival distillers, like Chivas Brothers. The Famous Grouse blended malt range came out of over-demand for The Macallan. They were done for markets like Taiwan in particular. Sales of them soared, and everyone else started to get in on the act, William Grant with Monkey Shoulder, Johnnie Walker with Gold Label and so on. They all suddenly hit the Taiwanese market.

'As Master Blender I had a Macallan team, which identified all the casks for a particular product – they drew samples and nosed them and produced a "bench" sample which was sent down to me in Glasgow for a final check. With new products I set the make-up and they put it together to that spec. For any single malt expression I would decide the spread of age and the cask types to be used. Max Macfarlane, "Whisky Maker" for Edrington, worked with me, and did lots of nosing. With Highland Park, we would get samples from casks and put together a bench sample if we needed to, at our head offices in Glasgow's Great Western Road.

'Every cask is nosed by somebody, both malts and grains. The grains would be nosed at the North British Distillery in Edinburgh, where the grain portion of our malts was all assembled. The nosers would be looking for any off-notes and judging the quality of the wood, considering whether these particular casks should be filled again. And the guys at most of the individual distilleries would be doing the same as the people at North British – checking for off-notes and future cask usage. They were all trained in sensory analysis to be able to do this.'

On a practical basis John says that, 'Mostly, the malt came in tankers from the various distilleries to Great Western Road for blending as Grouse and Cutty. We would vat all the malts together and get a sample of the malt element. We would then adjust that, if necessary. Then the grain element would be brought through from North British Distillery. We would take a sample of that mix, and then pump from the vat of malt into the grain vat, before adding water to take it down to around forty-five to forty-six per cent.

'This was then drawn off into casks for a period of marrying. Originally we married for six months, but this was obviously expensive, and we did experiments and found that in four to six weeks most of the desirable changes take place, so now we aim for two months as a general rule, though it does vary. Fundamentally, the blender works as he always has – it's about your nose. That never alters. You use your nose for quality control and your palate as well, to a greater extent, in new product development. Otherwise you're not using the palate much.

'These days there are twenty or more variants of The Macallan, ten or more of Highland Park, and ten of The Famous Grouse. Personally, I would drink a blend, probably The Famous Grouse Finest, most of the time, and maybe twelve-year-old Grouse Gold Reserve, or an aged malt after dinner.'

He adds that, 'On a personal level, a great achievement was winning the 2007 International Spirits Challenge Trophy for the thirty-year-old The Famous Grouse blended malt. The fact that it was a blended malt, rather than a single malt, gave me great pleasure. Blended malts are a challenge to create, but all in all, I prefer working with malts and grains.'

Like many of his fellow Master Blenders, John has served on the judging panels of a number of internationally significant awards, notably the International Spirits Challenge (ISC), and when it came to a final hurrah before retirement, John crafted a universally well-received expression of his pet project, The Glenrothes.

At the time, a Glenrothes spokesman said that, 'John has identified a parcel of second-fill American oak sherry casks from 1973 to 1987, which have now been married together and very gradually reduced in strength, but not chill-filtered. This limited edition of only fourteen hundred bottles will stand as John's legacy to The Glenrothes.'

Ronnie Cox, Brands Heritage Director, declared that, 'This exceptional bottling is a fitting tribute to one of the quiet men of blending; John lets his whiskies do the talking. I am confident "The Glenrothes John Ramsay" will prove to be an extremely articulate expression that will find favour with whisky enthusiasts everywhere.'

John himself closes with, 'My signature and tasting notes have been on each and every label of The Glenrothes since 2004. That final bottling gave me a wonderful opportunity to craft a single malt which embodied the exceptional quality and distinctive style of The Glenrothes and I was truly delighted with the result.'

PART FOUR
Keeping It In The Family

CHAPTER 11
John Grant – Distillery Owner

ALTHOUGH THOSE RESPONSIBLE FOR MARKETING Scotch whisky make much of the hand-crafted nature of the product, depicting it as made in small batches by devoted and long-serving employees for small, local companies, the modern Scotch whisky industry has actually developed along similar lines to most other manufacturing industries in Britain.

Its story is one of consolidation, rationalisation and globalisation of ownership. No fewer than 39 of the 98 malt distilleries operating in 2011 were in the possession of just two companies, namely Diageo and Pernod Ricard, and family-owned distilleries are rare creatures indeed.

In the whisky-making heartland of Speyside, the best-known name in independent distilling is that of William Grant & Sons Ltd, owners of the world's leading single malt Glenfiddich, from Dufftown. However, ten miles west along the A95 road towards Grantown-on-Spey is another privately owned whisky-making establishment, by the name of Glenfarclas.

Widely regarded as one of the great malt whiskies, Glenfarclas is noted for its significant use of ex-sherry casks for maturation. The distillery was established during 1836 in the shadow of Ben Rinnes. It takes its name from the Gaelic for 'glen of the green grassland,' and since 1865 has been in the hands of a branch of the Grant family unrelated to the Grants of Glenfiddich, today headed by chairman John Grant.

In many ways John confirms the impression one might have of an 'old school' distillery owner. It is impossible to imagine the imposing, smartly suited figure wearing jeans, and it soon becomes apparent during conversation that for him being a 'gentleman' is a very important attribute. A 'gentleman' should put on a good lunch for his guests, know his wines as well as his whiskies, and be generous with both. If he happens to own a spot of shooting and play a decent round of golf, then so much the better. John Grant represents the fifth generation of his family to own Glenfarclas, while his son George currently acts as brand ambassador for the single malt and offers the likelihood of continuing family ownership for some time to come.

John recalls that, 'My earliest memories of Glenfarclas Distillery are from the 1950s, when I was a boy. I was born in Aberdeen but was back at the distillery five days later and I was brought up here. So by the time I was five or six, I knew the distillery very well. There were lots of company houses on site, so there were more than a dozen kids here. There were my two sisters and me and all the staff families. The distillery was our playground, especially the malt barns!'

After leaving school John spent three years working for the Bank of Scotland, based in Edinburgh. 'That was probably much more use than university would have been. You learnt a lot in Leith in the late sixties! It was a thriving place then, with quite a few whisky companies like Macdonald and Muir, owners of Glenmorangie Distillery and the Highland Queen blend. Our customers included everyone from undertakers to publicans and I learnt a great deal about business in those three years.' There were, of course, trips back to Glenfarclas, where lessons in the potential perils of distillation could sometimes be learnt.

'At Hogmanay 1968 I was back up at Glenfarclas and a few of us had been celebrating quite lavishly. Eventually we decided to go down to the stillhouse in the early hours to wish the stillman, Jimmy Hill, a Good New Year.

'When we got there the sides of one of the wash stills were moving in and out. The stills were coal-fired at the time, of course. 'It's been on for three hours now and nothing's appeared in the spirit safe,' said a slightly bewildered Jimmy. Suddenly the still "blew" and we all dashed away and got every hose in the place and trained them on the hot copper. Someone was dispatched to inform the excise officer, who said "lock the door and we'll deal with it in the morning!" which wasn't like him at all.

'When we emptied the still next day we found that the copper in the bottom was only one-sixteenth-of-an-inch thick. We now carry a spare still bottom just in case we need it, and from then on the insurance company insisted we shut down for New Year!' After his spell as a banker, John took his first professional steps into the whisky industry, with his father, George, having arranged for him to take up employment with William Teacher & Sons Ltd. 'Like us, they were still a family company at that time. I was sent to Ardmore and to Glendronach, their two distilleries, not far from Huntly in Aberdeenshire, and I remember that I had never seen a whisky tanker before.

'They were tankering the whisky down to Glasgow for blending, once it had matured, and that saved a lot of wear and tear on casks and cut back on the lorry mileage. After being at the distilleries for a while I was based in Glasgow, and really I spent three years learning all aspects of how a relatively large blending company worked. I met a lot of nice people during my time there, too.

'I spent three months in each department, and I discovered that none of them really knew what the others did, they just knew there bit of the operation. I decided to make sure that didn't happen when I came back to Glenfarclas – that everybody was aware of everything that went on.'

John returned to Glenfarclas in 1974, just as production was slowing a little. 'We were on full production until 1971 to 72, and the "Old Man" [*his father*] could allocate stock to people for blending. They would be allocated so many hogsheads per year. 'In the early sixties my father had written in his diary that he could see mergers coming to the Scotch whisky industry; he could foresee rationalisation, and decided to keep back more of the distillery's output for himself, to lay down more stock each year with the aim of having a bottled single malt brand.

'It had first been bottled in the 1870s, but almost as a hobby, and it was only in 1959/60 that it was decided to do more single malt. It was bottled in Elgin by our own Grant Bonding Company, and our main market was the USA. At one time we may have been the number one single malt in the States, with sales of 3,000 to 4,000 cases per year. Because we were farmers we got a licence to distil throughout the Second World War, which meant that come the 1950s, we had stocks which we could sell in the USA.'

Back with the family firm at Glenfarclas, John found himself slightly surplus to requirements, noting that, 'We had a good distillery manager, so what exactly was I supposed to do? The "Old Man" told me to get out and sell whisky, which was not really something I knew about. I understood production.

'We had importers in the USA, Australia and New Zealand and Italy, so I bought a plane ticket to Christchurch in New Zealand, and stopped off in Palm Beach, in Alabama and Los Angeles. I arrived at our LA importer's house literally as he was being carried out in a coffin! In Australia I was coming up the escalator at Sydney airport as David Grant of William Grant and Sons was going down it, and he told me as we passed that they had just bought our Australian importers!'

However, matters improved from that point onwards, and John recalls that, 'The first importer I actually appointed myself was in Bordeaux, where I formed an association with Mahler-Besse. They were looking for a whisky to sell in France. They were already Teacher's agents in Belgium and they agreed to take twenty-five cases of Glenfarclas. Thirty-five years on we still have that relationship with them, only now they take it by the container load! It was all about word of mouth – the Mahler-Besse people had lots of contacts which they passed on to us and the snowball kept rolling. Today we export to fifty-five markets around the world.

'Our biggest markets are France, Germany, the UK and the USA. Ten years ago I'd have laughed at you if you had suggested it, but we now sell hundreds of thousands of cases to the Eastern Bloc each year. It's incredible how that market has opened up. India as a market has the advantage that English is widely spoken there. We've had a joint venture company in India for eleven years now, giving us a wee presence there.'

At the time when John rejoined his family distillery a major programme of reconstruction was under way. 'From 1973 to the end of 1976 we totally rebuilt the place, effectively creating a new distillery, with six stills rather than the previous four.

'We did our first mash when it was completed in 1976 and it was a disaster. It took three days for it to process, instead of a matter of hours, but by 1979 it was all worked out and everything was going well. We were doing fine until the early 1980s, when over-production in the industry came home to roost and the DCL closed more than twenty distilleries in 1983 and 1985.

'So what should we do? We decided just to carry on making whisky, and between 1982 and 1987 we kept building warehouses and filling them. We filled warehouses with spirit during the "great recession". And sure enough, come 1988 to 89, the phone started ringing with people desperate to get hold of four- and five-year-old whisky for blending. Filling levels increased but consolidation within the industry meant that we actually had fewer customers. In 1989 we paid off our overdraft and went into the black for the first time since 1896!'

John Grant's father, George, retired in 1979, at which point he became Managing Director. Comparing the way business is done within the Scotch whisky industry today, John says that, 'It's a different trade now to the one my father worked in. During the fifties, sixties and seventies people had been in the same jobs for years, there was more continuity, and there was lots more face-to-face contact, less phoning and obviously no emails. People like Duncan McGregor of Long John were almost like members of the family and it was all a lot more sociable. It was a more relaxed and gentlemanly way of doing business. When we installed our first computer in 1980 my father announced that he would retire!'

Despite the generational changes in the whisky industry, John declares that, 'There were still a lot of gentlemen in the trade during the eighties. Nineteen eighty-six was our 150th anniversary year and I was doing the rounds of our customers as usual. I went to see John Macphail of Highland Distillers, and when I told him what our prices were at that point he suggested I ask them for an extra few pence per litre. 'It's going to be an expensive year for you, after all,' he said. John was the only person who ever asked me to put my prices up! Even at that time, you would be asked by customers to turn up at eleven or eleven-thirty and stay for lunch, or at four or five pm and then go on for dinner after the meeting. People didn't want to see you at nine am.'

With John back at the family distillery in the mid-seventies, a concerted effort was made to market Glenfarclas as a single malt brand, and John notes that, 'By 1979 to 80 we had enough stock to offer a fifteen-year-old, by the mid-eighties a twenty-one-year-old, and by the late eighties, twenty-five and thirty-year-olds. Now we are able to have a forty-year-old as part of the current, permanent range. It's affordable because it's not over-packaged and we have lots of it. We make a reasonable margin, and I'd rather people drank it than collected it.'

John has firm views on the increasingly lavish way in which whisky is presented, declaring that, 'I think we should ban all secondary packaging, cartons, tubes and so on, from a carbon footprint point of view. If you buy a bottle of Chateau Latour or whatever, no matter how expensive and prestigious the wine, all you get is a bottle with a label. So why has the Scotch whisky industry gone down the route of using so much extravagant packaging?

'Our forty-year-old comes in a plain carton. It wouldn't even have that, none of our whiskies would, except that the marketing people say they must, in order to be competitive. The same applies to our Family Cask range.'

The Family Casks comprise a unique collection of the best single casks from the distillery's warehouses. Launched in 2007, the line-up initially comprised 43 single cask bottlings, with one cask from every year from 1952 to 1994. 'They aren't cheap, but I would say they represent fair value for money,' says John. 'It costs a lot to bottle a single cask. We do it because we have the stock, whereas many of our competitors don't. Simple as that.'

John's views on the advantages of Glenfarclas's much-lauded independence reflect those of many businessmen who are free to back their own judgement without fear or favour. 'We can take a long-term view and plan long-term strategies,' he explains. 'We aren't answerable to those terrible men in the City who are only interested in higher share prices and bigger dividends and don't care how it is achieved. We don't have that burden.

'During the eighties we were probably the only distillery in Scotland not to lay anybody off. Okay, some of the guys were put onto painting duties for a time and doing other maintenance work, but we didn't let anybody go. Many of the families, like our own, have been here for generations, and we feel a responsibility to them.

'The average length of employment here when I came back in the seventies was twenty-seven years, and though that has fallen quite a lot we don't have a high turnover of staff, and lots of the people working here are related to previous employees. We have three key employees based on site as part of their contracts. It's essentially a twenty-four-seven operation now and you have to have people here. I wouldn't be able to sleep at night otherwise.'

A total of eight of the old staff houses have been demolished, but some were constructed from iron and wood and dated back to 1911, while others were constructed with breeze blocks in the fifties. John does not rule out rebuilding some of the properties at a future date, and notes that, 'We have done up the oldest property on the site, a farmhouse, and the brewer lives there at the moment.'

While relatively large Scottish distilleries have become automated to the extent that one person can control an entire shift, this approach does not appeal to John, who says 'We have fourteen production staff, including the distillery manager. We have four people in sales and four in admin, plus two working full-time in the visitor centre, so around twenty-nine employees in total. We do all the administrative work for the company from the distillery, which adds to our staffing levels.'

Inevitably, when you have developed a brand on a global basis and it enjoys an extremely high reputation for quality and individuality, there is no shortage of people eager to acquire the business from you.

Perhaps the most eminent figure to attempt to purchase Glenfarclas was legendary Canadian-based distilling supremo Sam Bronfman, who headed the mighty Seagram Company Ltd. Bronfman's fortunes received a major boost during the period of US prohibition (1920-33) when he made large sums of money importing whisky into the USA from Canada, an operation facilitated by characters such as Chicago gangster Al Capone.

After the Second World War Seagram invested heavily in the Scotch whisky industry through its subsidiary Chivas Brothers Ltd, ultimately owning nine Scottish distilleries, including Strathisla, Longmorn, Glen Grant and The Glenlivet. The organisation developed the Chivas Regal blend into a global brand, favoured by high-profile figures such as Frank Sinatra and other members of the 'Rat Pack.'

John recalls that, 'We were once offered the proverbial blank cheque for the distillery. It Was around 1968, at Gleneagles Hotel in Perthshire. Sam Bronfman offered my father one million for the distillery, then five million when it was refused. Finally, he handed over the cheque book and pen to the old man and said, "Okay, just make it out yourself for whatever sum you want." I was there at the time and I remember wondering just how many noughts you could fit into the space! But my father just handed the cheque book and pen back to Sam and said, "Sorry, but it isn't for sale at any price." Despite that, we got a big order for fillings of Glenfarclas from Chivas Brothers. Sam Bronfman was a gentleman.'

Today, Scotch whisky distillers without a first-class sherried style of Speyside single malt in their portfolios continue to cast covetous eyes on Glenfarclas, and John notes that, 'I regularly get offers for the distillery; I had one just last year. But I just say no thank you. What would I do? I'm not greedy; I have a good lifestyle and a low boredom threshold. We are in charge of our destiny, because we do everything, including our own bottling. We own half of Broxburn Bottlers Ltd, bought in 1984 by us and Peter Russell of Ian Macleod Distillers.

'We have built the bottled brand, and it's great that we are no longer dependent on blenders for our survival, though we do still fill for blenders. We have a theoretical capacity of around three million litres per year, though we've never made that amount. We're doing a five-and-a-half to six-day week, making quantities we are happy with.'

Reflecting on the position of Glenfarclas in the wider world of Scotch whisky, John notes that, 'We are minnows in a huge ocean. Hopefully we are good members of the Scotch whisky trade. We behave ourselves, act responsibly and produce a quality, up-market product. We try to be good members of the community, too. The distillery will only be sold over my dead body, and I hope it will carry on after me. There are still great opportunities.'

Although Glenfarclas is a highly attractive prize for many rival distillers, John is not above contemplating acquisitions of his own. 'For years I was interested in buying the Black and White blend but I kept getting turned down. If a blended brand which was doing four to five thousand cases a year came along at the right price we could be interested. Also, I wouldn't rule out possibly buying another distillery if the right one came along.'

During his career in the Scotch whisky industry to date, Grant has seen many changes, but the most significant for him is the consolidation of the trade into ever fewer hands. 'I'm thinking of the creation of Diageo and the growth of Pernod Ricard by acquisitions,' he says. 'Who would have thought Seagram's, Allied Distillers, International Distillers and Vintners and so many other major names would have gone? And I'm sure there are still changes in terms of consolidation to come.'

Another change noted by Grant concerns production processes, and in particular the switch from direct-fired stills to internal steam heating, a practice which has been embraced by practically the whole industry, although Glenfarclas continues to directly fire its stills using gas burners. 'A lot of character has gone from actual whiskies,' he insists. 'With

Glenlivet, for example, the change from direct-fired to indirect was enormous. Just look at the samples. It's much more efficient, but different alcohols come off at different rates. You get slower heating when doing it internally, a more even distillation.

'We put a steam coil into one of our spirit stills for a few weeks – we borrowed it from Miltonduff – and what came out nosed bland. All the character and body and guts had gone. You definitely do get a different spirit. You get really individual character from direct-fired stills.'

Nobody can doubt the individual character of Glenfarclas, which competes with the likes of The Macallan and GlenDronach as relatively heavily sherried Speyside single malts. 'We have experimented with various types of wood and in 1973 to 74 we filled a dozen types of wood on the same day and put the casks together in the same warehouse. We filled fino, amontillado, oloroso and South African ex-sherries, plus a port pipe, an ex-bourbon cask and various others. We sampled them a few years later and they were all very different whiskies.

'From this exercise we decided oloroso sherry gave us the flavours we liked best, and for me using second-fill casks works better than first-fills. You get a nice, full-bodied whisky from the oloroso butts. We started buying sherry butts in 1978, and all our whisky has been natural in colour since 1990.'

Continuing to major in sherry-wood maturation while most competing distillers were switching to the widespread use of ex-bourbon casks has paid dividends for Glenfarclas, and any suggestion that his whisky is in any way 'old-fashioned' meets with short shrift from John.

'Sherried whiskies are emphatically not old-fashioned,' he insists. 'Just go to Taiwan and say that. They love the style in Asia. Yes, they are traditional, but they are very relevant and extremely popular in many global markets.'

In terms of cask selection, Grant is not a fan of the widespread practice of 'finishing' whisky in a secondary cask type, declaring that, 'I have never tasted a "finish" that is better than the original dram. Some of the finishes on offer have been appalling. It's either marketing men who are desperate or who have gone mad! Cragganmore is my favourite Diageo dram, but the port finish ruined it for me.'

Grant is not enamoured of the Islay style of medicinal spirit either, and explains that, 'Theoretically, I'm still banned from the island and until this year I hadn't been back since 1975. I was over playing golf at the Machrie that year and a *Sunday Times* journalist was staying at the hotel. He had been invited by the distillers on Islay, who had paid for him to visit with the intention of having him write a supplement about Islay whisky.

'However, he got very drunk in our company on the Saturday evening and finally found his way to bed in the early hours of Sunday, and proceeded to stay there until his flight to Glasgow was ready to leave on Monday morning. He didn't get to write anything about the distilleries and no supplement ever appeared. The Islay distillers were far from happy and they blamed me. I still have the letter they sent me, signed by representatives of all the distilleries, effectively saying I was not welcome back on the island!'

Along with the proliferation of cask finishes, another recent trend in the world of Scotch whisky has been for small-scale, 'craft' distilling ventures, and on this topic Grant says, 'Good luck to them if they can survive. It's not a business you come into to make a quick buck. You've got a big outlay for six to eight years and it's unlikely any of the blenders will buy big quantities of an unknown make. I wish them well, but will they be there in 25 years I wonder? Sadly, I think the future is in the Roseisles of this world, just big industrial units.'

Roseisle is just one of the latest in a line of some 20 new malt distilleries to have been constructed in Scotland since the end of the Second World War. However, John is unimpressed with the spirit, which is wholly destined for the blending vats. 'Not one of the distilleries built since the Second World War makes truly outstanding whisky,' he asserts. 'I would argue that none would be in any whisky drinker's top ten malts.'

Noting that in 2010 sales of Glenfarclas grew in volume by 26.7% over the previous year, and in terms of value to even greater level of growth, John says that, 'There has been a definite swing towards our older and more expensive products. Since the recession started, we have been doing really well. It's very strange.' Musing on life as one of the few chairmen of a family-owned Scotch whisky distilling business today, John concludes that, 'These are exciting times, though I think lots of fun has gone out of the business. But let's say we don't have a bad life!'

CHAPTER 12
Fred and Stewart Laing – Independent Bottlers

TODAY, WE TEND TO TAKE FOR granted the fact that major distillers spend large sums of money bottling and promoting their single malts, with leading players in the Scotch whisky industry like Diageo, Chivas Brothers, The Glenmorangie Company, William Grant & Sons and The Edrington Group working hard to market the various expressions of brands such as Cardhu, Talisker, The Glenlivet, Glenmorangie, Glenfiddich, The Macallan and Highland Park.

However, this is a relatively recent phenomenon, fuelled by the exceptional rise in the global profile of single malts during the past three decades. Once upon a time, very few producers bottled their own whiskies, with long-established companies like Gordon & MacPhail of Elgin on Speyside undertaking the bottling of a range of single malts on their behalf. Accordingly, Gordon & MacPhail became closely associated with distilleries such as Glen Grant, The Glenlivet and Strathisla.

Not only has the development of interest in malt whisky encouraged producers to bottle their own whiskies, but it has also seen a rise in the number of independent bottlers keen to capitalise on this new-found consumer interest. Venerable firms such as Gordon & MacPhail and Wm Cadenhead & Co have been joined by companies like Murray McDavid and Signatory, while other well-established but formerly low key enterprises have gained a new lease of life and a much higher profile of late. In this latter category is Glasgow-based Douglas Laing & Co, presided over by brothers and fellow directors Fred and Stewart Laing.

Fred says that, 'We were born Glasgow, and Fred Douglas was our father. In the thirties he was in shipping, and during the war he was an RAF sergeant operating radar in North Africa. After the war he met some Americans who owned the blended whisky brands House of Peers and King of Scots, and they had stocks of whisky for these blends. Initially they wanted our father to ship Scotch whisky for them to the USA and South America, but then he got into actually putting the blends together to their recipes. He was personally doing the blending.

'Then, in 1948 he bought the Americans out and started up on his own, with just the two brands and not much stock. So he had to establish contacts with distillers in order to be able to buy whisky, and in the early fifties he put his own "spec" of blended Scotch together. By starting his own filling programme, which is still carried on to this day, he developed a great nose and kept his notes in a "special book" which we still have.'

Stewart adds that, 'He had an office in Renfield Street, in the centre of Glasgow, on the corner of Drury Lane, and then moved to Robertson Street. He started doing an "admix" [*Scotch whisky which is exported in bulk and blended with locally produced spirit*] for Brazil that was big there, and one day he was sitting in his office unable to think of a name for it and he looked out of the window and saw the sign for Drury Street on the wall, so he called it Drury's.' Now part of the Campari Group, Drury's remains one of the best-known whiskies in Brazil.

Fred Laing Snr was operating at a time when the Scotch whisky industry was far less centralised, rationalised and monopolistic than is the case today, when several large distilling concerns dominate distillery and brand ownership, along with bulk sales. The pace of working life was less frenetic, and whisky brokers played a key role in buying and selling 'parcels' of whisky, principally for blending purposes. The brokers – 'the ten per cent men' as they were sometimes known – tended to be larger-than-life characters, such as Willie Lundie, George Christie and Gus Paterson, father of Whyte & Mackay's current, long-serving Master Blender, Richard Paterson.

'Our father did a bit of broking,' recalls Fred, 'but really saw himself as a brand builder. If he was tight on stocks he would deal with brokers like George Christie and Gus Paterson, who were real brokers. He was working with the DCL to buy stocks, along with Robertson and Baxter Ltd [*now part of The Edrington Group*] and Long John Distilleries. He had a good association with all of them.'

Fred Laing Snr enjoyed living in style, and Fred Jnr recalls that, 'He liked his Armstrong-Siddeley cars, his Jaguars and his Mercedes, and he would stay at the Savoy Hotel when he was in London. On business trips he would fly to New York on the BOAC Stratocruiser, which was a forerunner of the Jumbo jet. He was keen on horseracing, too, and liked the occasional bet. Like most people at the time he bet under a nom de plume [*off-course bookmaking was not legalised until 1960*], phoning the bookie and saying "Hello it's 'Jockey' here ... "

'Like a lot of guys who had seen service the war he was simply delighted to be alive – *carpe diem*, and all that. However, he was a very commercial and astute guy, though he liked his long lunches. They were part of the culture of the whisky business in Glasgow at the time. He would leave at noon perhaps for 101 or The Malmaison, which were two of the favoured

Glasgow restaurants, to meet his chums, like Gus Paterson and George Christie. And we might see him home at eight pm, pleasantly intoxicated, having done what everyone did in those days – driven home from the restaurant. I guess there was probably only the odd tram to miss!'

When it came to career choices for the young Fred and Stewart, there was little chance that they would fail to follow their father's chosen career. 'I am the elder son, so I left school first,' says Stewart, 'and I think our father had the philosophy that he knew his sons would make mistakes and he wanted them made at someone else's expense.

'One of my mother and father's great friends was Sandy Grant, of A and B Grant and Co, who owned Bruichladdich and Bladnoch distilleries in the sixties. So I trained at Bruichladdich on the island of Islay in the summer of 1966. The seamen's strike was on at the time so I couldn't have left if I wanted to, but I didn't want to because I loved the place. I did a bit of everything, from working in the warehouses to running the stills. I have to say that Bruichladdich hasn't changed very much at all since my time there.'

Sandy Grant is the subject of one of Fred's favourite stories, which he tells while brother Stewart listens with a smile. 'Sandy was great friends of mum and dad,' he says. 'Sandy drove a Rolls-Royce and co-owned "bits" of racehorses with father. Sadly, he and his wife couldn't have children, and one night in the late fifties the two couples were having dinner. Suddenly, after a few glasses of wine and a number of drams had been consumed, Sandy suggested that he would like to swap Bruichladdich for "wee Freddy". Dad was apparently about to pounce on the deal when our mother intervened. Stewart is still annoyed that the exchange didn't happen!'

After his training at the 'sharp end' at Bruichladdich, Stewart joined Stevenson Taylor & Co, a wine and spirits company, learning about the commercial side of the Scotch whisky industry. 'After that, I went back to work for my father,' he says. 'He had a bottling hall downstairs in his place on Robertson Street, and in the Railway Bond on Bell Street. I became involved with the bottling side of things.'

Brother Fred recalls that, 'Father steered me towards the University of Life, instead of university, and he did it quite forcefully, really. I got a trainee apprenticeship with Whyte and Mackay, one of the major independent Glasgow distillers at the time, and it was still run by Major Hartley Whyte and his brother, Alex.

'The Major was a remarkable figure, with a luxuriant, white moustache, and a habit of wearing plus-fours. He had a collection of vintage cars and he knew everybody. In the company's old offices in Wellington Street in Glasgow there were photographs of him playing golf with Clark Gable, arm-in-arm with Marilyn Monroe, having lunch with Trevor Howard, and so on. He was very clever at opening up markets in the States for Whyte and Mackay, and was clearly adept at "pressing the flesh".'

After this initial grounding in the Scotch whisky business, Fred spent some time working with White Horse Distillers, a subsidiary of DCL. 'After that, I joined Stewart and dad in 1972. I came in partly to free up Stewart to get more into the sales side of things. I got involved with production, and it allowed us to expand. During the industrial disputes of 1976 we loaded up trucks with bottles ourselves and ran the picket lines to get supplies of glassware, and we even hand-labelled bottles when we had to at that time.'

Having been perceived as what Stewart Laing calls 'cheap and cheerful' during the early to mid-1970s, Douglas Laing & Co Ltd moved into the duty-free arena, and Fred recalls that, 'We saw that the French Cognac houses were putting their old Cognacs into really good packaging. The King of Scots blend had a fabulous name, and we went about packaging it well for the duty-free market.

'We started to use some of the older stock we had and launched King of Scots Rare Extra Old and seventeen and twenty-one-year-old versions for duty-free in the Far East. From the early 1980s onwards we were selling lots of whisky in the Pacific Rim area, and I even crammed a Japanese language course at night school to help our sales there. Ultimately, we got into even fancier packaging. Everybody was using ceramics and crystal decanters, with parchment scrolls and wooden boxes. Fancy packaging was big in the the Far East markets then and still is today.'

In addition to the King of Scots range, Laing's also produced another eye-catching bottling, this time for Imperial Tobacco, namely the John Player Special or JPS blended whisky. 'Today, tobacco and whisky aren't really seen as a good mix,' admits Fred, 'but I remember the black and gold JPS Lotus Formula 1 racing cars, driven by people like Emerson Fittipaldi and Ayrton Senna and they looked amazing.'

As involvement with Pacific Rim markets had developed, less attention was paid by the Laing's to Europe and North America, and as Stewart recalls, 'When the so-called "tiger" economies [*Japan, South Korea, Thailand and Taiwan*] had problems in the mid-1990s we were hit by that.

'We had piled up stocks of old whiskies for blending for the Pacific Rim markets, where we were doing thirty and thirty-five-year-old blends, so we were severely exposed. We couldn't put the same blends into Europe or the USA, because they just weren't the right product; the really old blends appealed to countries in Asia.'

It was out of apparent adversity at this point that the Laing brothers hit on the idea that was to transform the profile of the company's product lines. Fred says that, 'We hadn't actually blended those stocks of old whiskies, so we decided, with some trepidation, to market them as single-cask bottlings. We knew it was a potential nightmare, being such a change in scale for us, down from thousands of cases to perhaps just 350 bottles.

'We had twenty-five, twenty-six and twenty-seven-year-old Ardbegs, old Macallans, Port Ellens and Laphroaigs, to name but a few. We began to release whiskies under the Old Malt Cask label in 1998. We were releasing mid-twenties to early thirty-year-old whiskies at prices that helped establish the range.'

Before long, Douglas Laing & Co was perceived as a 'second string' independent bottler behind the likes of Gordon & MacPhail and the energetic newcomer Signatory Vintage Scotch Whisky, established in 1998 by Andrew and Brian Symington.

Fred notes that, 'The Urquhart family, which owns Gordon and MacPhail, and Andrew Symington had "seeded" the market by teaching people about the single malt category and, in a way, we rode their coat-tails. We really prefer to build from nothing, as it were, to create, and the single cask bottlings didn't involve us in blending or anything. It was purely cask selection.'

The initial batch of releases included Auchroisk, Caol Ila and a 31-year-old Oban, all brands owned by Diageo. Turnbull Hutton, the industry giant's Scottish production director, a gloriously politically incorrect and expletive-ridden character, subsequently 'requested' that the Laings refrained from bottling any more of Diageo's Classic Malts, such as Oban.

Diageo had invested heavily in marketing this regionally representative range of six single malts, and were understandably reluctant to see independent, and perhaps 'rogue' bottlings of those brands, hitting the shelves. They had no control over the quality of the product, and there was no guarantee that all independent bottlers have been as professional and scrupulous as the Laing brothers.

'We had stocks of Oban and another Classic Malt, Cragganmore,' says Fred, 'but we agreed not to bottle any more as single casks. Another distiller who didn't like what we were doing very much was John Grant of Glenfarclas, who had just fought Cadenhead's in the USA over use of the Glenfarclas name and he had won the court case. Eventually, we settled on bottling our Glenfarclas as "Distilled at probably the best distillery on Speyside"!

'We have a second "home" for casks that are good, but not good enough for Old Malt Cask bottlings, as we can use them in our blends. Quantity-wise we sell more blends than malts, though the blends are trailing off a bit, but they are still very important in giving us volume sales.'

In addition to the Old Malt Cask line up, bottled at the Laing brothers' preferred strength of 50%abv, the company also produce what Fred refers to as, 'The big brother to Old Malt Cask,' namely Old & Rare Platinum Selection which comprises cask-strength bottlings, along with several other ranges. Today, there are probably more than 100 different expressions of Douglas Laing whisky available at any one time, with ages varying from 10 up to 45 years old.

Noting the hands-on nature of their business, Fred points out that, 'Two or three times a week Stewart and I go through cask samples, deciding on what will go into future bottlings.' He jokes that, 'If I've been swallowing the samples to get a real sense of the palate and finish, I can occasionally be quite relaxed by around nine-thirty in the morning!'

A perennial favourite among the company's bottlings is the cult Islay malt of Port Ellen, which is invariably one of the most popular offerings from any defunct distillery, whichever independent bottler produces it. Port Ellen was one of the distilleries to be axed by the DCL in 1983, and according to Stewart, 'It was our father's favourite whisky. We removed it from our blending programme to keep it for single cask bottlings, and increasing the price doesn't slow sales down! The characteristic old, soft, chewed leather appeals to consumers, and people like the closed distillery aspect. It's popular with collectors.'

Fred notes that, 'Without naming names, some distilleries past and present haven't always had great reputations for their single malts, but even if the reputation of a distillery wasn't good we would release a bottling it if we had a particularly fine cask from it.

'We compete with the opposition in terms of independent bottlers partly by reputation, partly because Stewart and I as brand owners are regularly out there in the market place, and also because people know we have big stocks of old whisky, we're not just out there buying whatever we can. Ultimately, we are competing on the basis of the last bottle bought by the consumer.'

The switch from being principally a purveyor of blends to a specialist small-batch bottler has changed the profile of trading territories for the Laing brothers, and Stewart says that, 'The UK is now our biggest market, and if you'd told father that would be the case one day, he wouldn't have believed you. We never sold in the UK until ten or eleven years ago. After the UK there are Taiwan and Japan, both high-value markets. Germany, France and Scandinavia are important, too. I enjoy going to Japan, New Zealand and Australia in particular. Usually it's principally work, and we don't get much time for anything else, but in China I will go sightseeing. I'm fascinated by the country.

'There is obviously a far greater interest in malts now than there ever was, and it's exciting to go into a country like Finland, which is just getting into malts. Traditionally, it's a Cognac country. People like the depth and breadth of flavours of Scotch whisky and the great story of the spirit and its history. I love to be part of that. Overall, there's a much greater level of knowledge we find now. People love the country, its history, and the actual drink itself. I am privileged to be involved. We feel the benefits of everything that people in the past, including our father, have done for Scotch whisky.'

As well as the change of direction taken by the Laings, the wider whisky industry 'landscape' has altered significantly. Stewart says that, 'The biggest change since I started in the whisky business in 1964 is that there are far fewer companies. So many of the small ones have gone or have been amalgamated into bigger concerns. The industry is much bigger, but with far fewer players. Dad wouldn't recognise the industry today.'

Glasgow, in the west, vied with Edinburgh's Port of Leith, in the east, as a centre for the Scotch whisky industry's warehousing, blending, bottling and administration facilities, and this trade on the Clyde owed much to the fact that in the early 19th century the river was dredged, enabling large ships to dock relatively close to the city centre. During the 1830s, Glasgow became an important centre for the importation of tobacco and tea, and of the 80 warehouses listed in an 1830s edition of the *Glasgow Post Office Directory*, ten offered bonding facilities for spirits.

'Lots of the Glasgow companies have gone now,' says Fred. 'We were in Robertson Street and Cheapside, and that whole area close to the Clyde was a centre for the whisky trade in Glasgow, because historically lots of malt whisky came into Glasgow by boat from distant distilleries and was landed at the Broomielaw. William Whiteley, who owned the House of Lords blend and James Buchanan, who produced Black and White, were both in that area. Buchanan's had cart horses which pulled big drays around Glasgow when we were boys.'

Today, only Chivas Brothers' Strathclyde grain distillery, situated next to the Clyde in the Gorbals district, links Glasgow directly with whisky-making, though Whyte & Mackay Ltd continues to have its headquarters in the city, and several major bottling and warehousing establishments are located within the area.

Glasgow's second grain distillery, Port Dundas, closed in 2010, and with its demolition, Fred was forced to find a new 'parlour game' for visitors to his firm's offices in a stylish crescent in the Park area of the city, which dates from the 1860s. There, a comfortable and unpretentious room on the top floor of the building serves as an unofficial tasting area, in what Stewart Laing says ' ... used to be the servants' quarters.'

He has long had a habit of asking visitors which distillery it is that they can see from the window, and very few have ever answered correctly. However, with the site being cleared for future redevelopment, the distinctive distillery structures and chimney will soon be lost to the Glasgow skyline. The heritage of Scotch whisky is constantly shifting, and what was current one day may become historic the next, after a few hours' work with a wrecking ball.

Whatever physical changes may occur, however, the stories remain. Fred recalls that the Ugandan dictator Idi Amin was educated at the Royal Military Academy, Sandhurst, and in the mid-1970s became a general in his native Uganda, going on to command the Ugandan army before seizing power in a military coup during 1971.

'He declared that, "Scots do not need a visa to visit our country," proclaiming himself "King of Scots" in his kilt in the sweltering heat of Kampala,' says Fred. 'We saw this as a golden opportunity and wrote to him, saying that he should be drinking King of Scots whisky, and after a while we got a letter with a cheque enclosed from Amin, and this was the start of quite a big trade in our King of Scots blend, which Amin dished out to the troops and to members of the police force.'

Fred describes himself as 'A huge Rolling Stones fan, and I love rock from the 1960s, but I also enjoy modern American Indy rock bands like the Killers.' The perils of being 'frontman' for the company, to use a rock analogy, have included being involved in a brawl in Phnom Penh, Cambodia, ' ... in a bar where customers were required to leave their guns in a shoebox at the door. On another occasion I was arrested in Moscow's Red Square for looking like a Chechen rebel. Well, I did have a beard at the time. I was also once mistaken for Mick Jagger in Taipei, Taiwan, when I was doing karaoke because I was word perfect in *Satisfaction* and did all the moves as well!'

Away from work, the Laing brothers have contrasting approaches to leisure, with Stewart saying, 'I enjoy watching football and walking my dogs in the countryside. It's a great way of clearing my head away from the phone and emails of work.'

Fred declares that, 'Like my brother, I also watch football and rugby, but in terms of sport, I prefer to participate rather than watch. My aim is to gain an international over-sixties squash cap for Scotland. I have beaten the captain, so it may happen. I also play racket ball, ski and go to the gym regularly. I have a personal trainer who comes to the house sometimes, and in order to go through the pain barrier I need good rock music as I'm exercising.'

When it comes to a relaxing dram, Stewart notes that, 'The first single malt I ever really liked and got into was a sherry cask North Port, distilled in Brechin,' proving the point that even a distillery not usually considered in the first rank can turn out memorable whisky.

Fred says that, 'I love honey and sherry flavours, but the emotional tie with Port Ellen, my father's favourite whisky, makes it mine too. My "desert-island dram" would be from an early sherry cask of Port Ellen. Ex-sherry wood brings fruit and raisins, beyond the usual soft smack of chewed leather.'

Recalling the lengthy lunches that characterised the whisky industry in Glasgow during less pressured times, he adds that, 'After "the lunch" had finished late in the afternoon my father would go back to the office to sign some letters and carry on the party, as it were, with a few drams of Port Ellen. By the time he got home I was usually in bed, and he would wake me up to ask about my day at school and I would smell this wonderful alcoholic breath!

'It was probably forty years later, twenty years after his death in 1984, when I was conducting a whisky tasting one day and I got a whiff of Port Ellen with its leathery sweep of saline, beaches and dry ropes. It took me straight back to those days when I was a child and it was a very emotional moment.'